Teaching Thinking Skills Across the Primary Curriculum

A practical approach for all abilities

Edited by

Belle Wallace

David Fulton Publishers
London

in association with
The National Association for Able Children in Education

David Fulton Publishers Ltd
Ormond House, 26–27 Boswell Street, London WC1N 3JZ

www.fultonpublishers.co.uk

First published in Great Britain by David Fulton Publishers 2001
Reprinted 2002

Note: The right of Belle Wallace to be identified as the editor of this work has been asserted by her in accordance with the Copyright, Designs and Patents Act 1988.

British Library Cataloguing in Publication Data
A catalogue record for this book is available from the British Library

ISBN 1–85346–766–9

Designed and typeset by Kate Williams, Abergavenny
Printed in Great Britain by Bell and Bain Ltd, Glasgow

Contents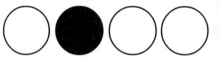

Notes on Contributors

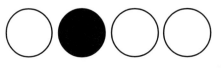

Chris Barrett has acquired a wide range of teaching experiences in secondary, middle, junior and primary schools. For the past 10 years he has been the head teacher at William Hildyard Primary School, Lincolnshire. He has always had a deep interest in the development of children's problem-solving and thinking skills, particularly in mathematics. During the academic year 1999/2000 he was seconded as an advisory teacher for mathematics and was able to pursue and develop his major interest.

Nicola Beverley has been a Curriculum Advisor for Primary Science in Lincolnshire for five years. She provides support to schools in the overall development of the science curriculum, and also to individual teachers seeking to extend their personal knowledge and understanding in science, together with their classroom management skills. As an active member of the Association for Science Education (section and regional committees) she is actively involved in raising the profile of science throughout the East Midlands.

Diana Cave began her teaching career in middle schools in Warwickshire and for the past 13 years has taught in The National School, Lincolnshire. During this time she has held a number of consecutive posts with special responsibility, namely: Year 3 Team Leader coordinating work across the year and liaising with local

infant schools; Year 6 Team Leader; Assessment Coordinator and Curriculum Coordinator. She has consequently acquired a unique range of experience across both subject areas and year groups.

Graduating in Geography from Queen Mary College, London, **Victoria Honeywood** has gained wide experience teaching in Norfolk, Suffolk, Cambridgeshire and Lincolnshire. She has a special interest in the teaching of problem-solving and thinking skills and currently divides her time between the development of thinking skills activities for classroom use and parenting three young sons.

Nina Spilsbury began her teaching career in Wolverhampton in primary schools. She then joined a team of advisors developing Multicultural Education across the LEA. Moving to Lincolnshire, she worked for a brief time in secondary schools teaching children with special educational needs. She then helped to establish two new initiatives: one for children with English as an additional language and the second, a reading recovery programme. For three years she worked as a Literacy Advisor but has recently chosen to return to the classroom.

Belle Wallace has worked with very able children for 25 years: first in an advisory capacity to Essex schools; and then as a researcher and developer of a problem-solving and thinking skills base for curriculum development. Since its inception in 1982, she has been editor of the journal *Gifted Education International*. She has published widely, served on the Executive Board of the World Council for Gifted and Talented Children, and given key-note lectures nationally and internationally. Her particular interest is in working with teachers to develop their expertise in the teaching of problem-solving and thinking skills through the curriculum.

Acknowledgements ○●○○

My special thanks to Harvey B. Adams, since we have worked together over many years to research a generic and sound theoretical framework for the development of problem-solving and thinking skills across the curriculum. His incisive ideas and generosity of time have helped to clarify my thinking and without his contribution to its formative development, this book would not have been written.

My thanks also to Christopher Barrett, Nicola Beverley, Diana Cave, Victoria Honeywood and Nina Spilsbury: they have worked creatively and collaboratively to share their wide experience and expertise with colleagues in the teaching profession. A theoretical framework about how children best learn is only useful if it generates good practice, and the co-writers have contributed ideas with the reality of the classroom in the forefront of their minds.

Thanks, too, to all the teachers who have been members of the wider school groups: they have trialled ideas and supported all the writers by being so willing to spend extra hours in preparation and evaluative discussion. Their commitment to the children in their care is generated from genuine concern, dedication and professionalism.

Thanks to the following schools for their cooperation: Boston West Primary, Chestnut Street Primary, Corby Glen Primary School, The National School, North Kelsey Primary, Usher School, William Hildyard School.

And, finally, thanks to the children who have responded with the excited willingness to explore new ideas that is so wonderful in the young: it is the gift which all children have and which makes creative teaching such a joy.

Belle Wallace
May 2001

For Teachers, Parents and Children

As teachers and parents, we want all children to extend and maximise their potential: we want all children to be the best that they can be and to live life as fully as they can. All children are born with the gift for learning, with a natural curiosity and drive to find things out for themselves, and, as adults, we know that these natural gifts need stimulating and nourishing both at home and at school if children are to be the best that they can be.

How do we provide this stimulation and encouragement? We all know that the greatest help we can offer to children lies in building their confidence and self-esteem; supporting them while they try new experiences; teaching them to use their curiosity and to question; spending time to talk and explore; and, most importantly, teaching them how to think and solve problems.

Recent research worldwide shows us that intelligence is not a static commodity that we inherit as a fixed package: our intellectual capacity can be diminished or strengthened and decreased or increased by the experiences we have and the kind of teaching and mentoring we receive. We can all actively develop our minds and although, as adults, we can continue to develop our mental capacities, children are particularly receptive to 'training their brain power'. All children can acquire 'learning how to learn' skills; all children can practise and get better at using problem-solving and thinking skills. All we need

to do is teach them in a problem-solving and thinking skills way! When we model thinking skills and strategies in the classroom, then we are providing a thinking framework or 'scaffolding' for young learners to follow. This not only supports the slower learners but also allows the faster learners to develop the skills they need for independent or small group work.

Although, as teachers and parents, we would say that of course we encourage the children in our care *to think*, this book has been written with the intention of increasing our awareness of how to do it better. There are teaching techniques and strategies we can perfect, professional understandings we need to have, practical skills we need to teach, kinds of questions we need to ask, and general classroom approaches we need to adopt. With regard to the children's development, they need to practise and perfect a range of problem-solving and thinking skills until they have complete confidence in using them across the curriculum and in real-life situations.

This means not only embedding the skills in relevant curriculum and life contexts but also finding ways to link the more 'unusual' areas of the National Curriculum to the interests and experiences of the children. Children learn best by extending from the base of what they already know, and by linking and hooking all new knowledge into their existing mental framework, they can actively develop new mental pathways. However, it is not enough just to increase children's knowledge base; they need to be using their knowledge to solve problems and pursue investigations and we can teach them the relevant skills to do this.

But we must never forget that children develop at varying rates and, even if it were possible to provide the perfect environment at home and in school, all children have a varying cluster of inherited characteristics: they have a range of strengths and weaknesses. Moreover, as parents we have one child or, maybe, a few children to care for: as teachers we have 30 or more children to care for! And we all recognise that teachers have an exhausting task!

However, if parents and teachers work together, try to understand each other's problems, are open in communication, are willing to co-operate and are reluctant to be overly critical and demanding, then we stand a chance of meeting the most important needs of the children who will be the problem-solvers of tomorrow.

Our common agreement must be to wear each other's shoes for a while and walk along the way together. Our common purpose must be to complement the work and effort of each other. Our common goal must be to do the best we can, accepting that we are all fallible and imperfect. Our common understanding must acknowledge that the children in our care are also fallible and imperfect and that whether we are parents or teachers, we cannot produce perfect young adults: we can only assist and support as best we can.

This book is dedicated to those who are ready to walk together down a demanding and rocky road.

Introduction ○●○○

We all know from experience that the acquisition of knowledge is useless mental baggage unless we use and apply it in our thinking and problem-solving. How much inert knowledge have we all memorised and then forgotten after 'the test'? How much of the knowledge we learned in school is remembered in adulthood as a patchwork of faded and hazy bits of this and that? When we were young learners, how much time did we and our teachers waste on the mechanical classroom exchange of scribbling down and parroting back pages of notes? As professional and creative teachers, we all seek to avoid perpetuating the negative learning experiences of our youth; and we all seek to promote the exhilarating, energising experiences that fired our enthusiasm and opened avenues of new exploration and interest. The teachers we remember are those creative teachers who inspired us to go further; and we will be remembered by our pupils for the same reason. Our pupils will talk about the teachers who enabled them to learn, who interacted and challenged thinking.

The Department for Education and Employment (DfEE) has been urging us that we need to promote higher standards in our classes, and the Minister for Education, David Blunkett, has also stressed the importance of teaching children how to think. But both as teachers and parents, we would say that we have always been concerned that our children *attained good standards* and *thought for themselves,* so what is new?

First, perhaps we need to sharpen our awareness of how we can systematically teach all children the skills of problem-solving and efficient thinking. In the light of recent worldwide research into how we develop children's thinking, there is a new awareness of how the brain works when it is functioning efficiently. Secondly, there is wide acceptance that 'intelligence' is not fixed and that the level of all children's mental capacity can be enhanced through appropriate intervention and teaching techniques.

Selecting appropriate content as the vehicle for problem-solving and thinking is obviously very important, and linking that content to the learner's experience is essential. We know that our active knowledge forms the basis for our mental activity: we all know that the repertoire of knowledge that we *understand* and *use regularly* for our thinking remains in our active working memory. Of course, we can learn some things by rote and through practice – shorthand tools like mathematics tables, a memorised repertoire of words we use regularly, technical skills – but even this learning has to be immersed within a relevant context and not a meaningless drill.

Consequently, the aim of this book is to target the issues of developing problem-solving and thinking skills across the National Curriculum. The intended outcomes are to:

- provide an accessible and practical 'hands on' manual of ideas for teachers and parents to use in order to develop children's thinking capacity;
- provide guidance on how to extend the current work being carried out in schools in an incremental and time-effective way, so that standards are raised across the whole school;
- share practical ideas that have been developed by teachers for teachers;
- show examples of children's work developed from a problem-solving and thinking skills framework;
- provide a brief theoretical base for the teaching of problem-solving and thinking skills as a grounding from which sound practice can be justified and developed;
- present information that is quickly absorbed through a series of mindmaps that give an overview of important points for planning and decision-making.

THE NATIONAL ASSOCIATION FOR ABLE CHILDREN IN EDUCATION
PO Box 242, Arnolds Way,
Oxford OX2 9FR

Registered Charity No. 327230

Tel: 01865 861879
e-mail: info@nace.co.uk

Fax: 01865 861880
www.nace.co.uk

MISSION STATEMENT

NACE . . . the association of professionals, promoting and supporting the education of able and talented children.

AIMS

1. To promote the fact that able and talented children have particular educational needs that must be met to realise their full potential.
2. To be proactive in promoting discussion and debate by raising appropriate issues in all education forums and through liaison with educational policy makers.
3. To encourage commitment to the personal, social and intellectual development of the whole child.
4. To encourage a broad, balanced and appropriate curriculum for able and talented children.
5. To encourage the use of a differentiated educational provision in the classroom through curriculum enrichment and extension.
6. To make education an enjoyable, exciting and worthwhile experience for the able and talented child.

OBJECTIVES

1. To promote the development, implementation and evaluation in all schools of a coherent policy for able and talented children.
2. To provide appropriate support, resources and materials for the education of able and talented children.
3. To provide methods of identification and support to the education community.
4. To provide and facilitate appropriate initial teacher training.
5. To stimulate, initiate and coordinate research activities.
6. To develop a national base and establish regional centres.

STATEMENT

To make education an enjoyable, exciting and worthwhile experience for able and talented children.

The National Association for Able Children in Education

In-service Training Provision

Our trainers can provide INSET for individual schools, clusters or partnerships of schools, LEAs and Professional Development Centres.

COST PER DAY
FROM
£400
PLUS VAT
A CHARGE OF 25p
PER MILE WILL BE MADE
FOR TRAINER'S TRAVEL
PLUS SUBSISTENCE
WHEN AN OVERNIGHT STAY
HAS BEEN NECESSARY

Did you know that 1 in 5 of your pupils is able and talented?

Call us to discuss the focus of your INSET

NACE
PO Box 242, Arnolds Way,
Oxford OX2 9FR

Tel: 01865 861879
Fax: 01865 861880

E-mail: info@nace.co.uk
www.nace.co.uk

The National Association for Able Children in Education

Registered Charity No. 327230   VAT No. 536 5807 26

So What's New About Teaching Children to Think?

BELLE WALLACE

*My thought is me: that's why I can't stop. I exist by
what I think . . . and I can't prevent myself from thinking.*
J.-P. Sartre, *La Nausee* (1938), 'Lundi'

PURPOSE

The purpose of this section is to explore some issues raised in the
many debates over what is meant when we are urged to teach children
to think. All of us would argue that 'thinking' is the natural and
automatic response of human beings to their environment. So why
do we need to be urged to develop 'thinking' in our classrooms? What's
new?

GROUP DISCUSSION

Reflect on the following comments and decide whether you agree or
disagree with what is being said. Add your own ideas to the collection of thoughts and opinions.

> I have always been
> concerned to develop thinking
> in my classes. I constantly ask
> questions to make sure the
> pupils understand.

> Yes, we agree that teachers are
> concerned that pupils are thinking, but
> perhaps there is a need to examine and
> sharpen our classroom practice. More
> than ever before, the complexity of
> modern life demands problem-solving
> and thinking skills.

But only the brightest pupils will ever be capable of logical, independent thinking. Most pupils need to be encouraged to adopt desirable modes of thinking so that they understand the accepted rules of a decent society.

Intelligence is not a fixed commodity in any individual and with appropriate teaching, all individuals can improve their capacity to think and solve problems for themselves. With help, all individuals are capable of reasoned decision-making. Modelling thinking skills in the classroom not only supports the slower learners but provides the faster learners with skills they need to work independently or in a small group.

But some children are born with an innate capacity to solve problems. It's in their genes and they thrive on it!

Certainly, we are all genetically different but a good 'thinking skills diet' helps us to maximise our mental potential just as a good 'food diet' maximises our physical potential. It's getting the right balance between 'nature' and 'nurture' that's critical. It's also a question of actively developing the mind through using appropriate teaching and learning strategies — teaching the pupils 'how' to think, not 'what' to think.

Some people recommend special lessons for the teaching of problem-solving and thinking skills — once a week, perhaps, as an extra subject.

Well, you can't stick thinking skills on like an elastoplast! Our mental skills develop when we are engrossed in thinking and solving problems that are real and relevant to our lives. We need to embed the skills in context and then reflect on our thinking processes and deliberately work towards transferring those skills into a different context.

Not everything we are expected to teach in the National Curriculum is relevant to the learners' lives!

No, it isn't immediately relevant, but, as good teachers, we need to find the links with real life as a way into the content. And we need to present as much content as is possible as a problem to be solved — a dilemma in history, a crisis in a novel, an environmental problem in geography, an examination of evidence in science.

Some things need to be taught directly and some skills need to be practised. It can't be all problem-solving and thinking skills.

No, it can't. Nor is this desirable. The way we learn needs a balance of direct teaching, demonstration, practice, rote learning and problem-solving. When a young child is learning to read, there must be practice, but the concentration needed to decode and understand is much easier if the story is exciting: and the patience needed to practise writing is made easier if there is a real purpose behind it and a real audience to share it with.

Our thinking processes develop with maturity and experience so why do we need special teaching?

Yes, we do learn by experience but if we have a good model to follow, we make faster progress and we learn more easily. A teacher who shares her thinking processes with her pupils is modelling thinking. The senior learner is inducting the apprentice junior learner into the different styles of thinking: the learner then practises until she or he has gained competency and can manage to use the strategies without help.

Is it important to have a consistent approach to the teaching of problem-solving and thinking skills across the curriculum? Should there be a whole-school policy? And, surely some subjects in the curriculum have 'subject-specific' skills.

There is a generic core of thinking skills and strategies which constitute a broad problem-solving approach within all subjects. And there are also subject-specific skills such as ways of organising mathematical thinking, writing poetry or recording a science experiment. A whole-school approach to the development of the generic core of skills, however, gives consistency across the curriculum and, consequently, skills are more easily transferred across subjects.

What do you think?

Reflect for a while about the importance of teaching children a range of problem-solving and thinking skills. Undoubtedly, we all try to incorporate strategies for teaching 'thinking' into our lessons already. Perhaps we can extend and consolidate what we are doing. Perhaps we need to strengthen the ways we teach 'learning how to learn' skills.

Remember that any developmental change in our classroom practice takes time to consolidate!

So often we say, 'But I taught the pupils how to do that in a numeracy lesson only a month ago!' And we constantly complain that the skills we taught in mathematics seldom transfer to science or geography or that the skills of using punctuation haven't transferred to other areas of the curriculum.

Perhaps we can improve our 'teaching for transfer of skills' and so save a lot of time and effort.

Why do so many children 'forget' what we thought they knew? Why do we need to say the same things over and over again? Why do we need to give constant reminders?

Perhaps we need to help the children to crystallise what they know and can do. Perhaps we need to spend more time reflecting on what skills they are developing.

Recently, there has been a surge of government interest in the teaching of thinking and problem-solving skills and schools are being asked to target the development of these skills across the curriculum. It is apparent that many pupils are failing to reach the higher levels of the National Curriculum and this is particularly apparent with regard to very able pupils who should be attaining the highest levels. It is suggested that the reason for this is that pupils cannot cope with the higher order questions, which need problem-solving approaches (Office for Standards in Education (OFSTED) 1994). However, we would stress very strongly that 'problem-solving and thinking skills' are not only for very able children: *when all children are taught how to use a range of thinking and problem-solving skills and strategies, then all children's attainment levels rise.*

So, as teachers and parents, we need to audit what we are currently doing with regard to the development of pupils' capacities to use thinking and problem-solving skills. And the audit should involve both home and school practice, since the education of the young should be a working partnership between parents and teachers. It is important to emphasise again that extending and consolidating a thinking skills and problem-solving approach to the curriculum supports the less able in the development of their potential by giving them the framework for the mental 'scaffolding' they need. At the same time, the more able rapidly acquire the skills they need for independent

and group activities. However, classroom work that systematically develops thinking does encourage and promote greater differentiation of pupil response but when the ethos of the class is that everyone matters and everyone has both strengths and weaknesses, then it is OK to be different and to show varying abilities.

Theoretical background to the model of problem-solving and thinking skills used throughout this text

In the mid-1980s, Belle Wallace and Harvey B. Adams surveyed the main thinking skills packages that were already published and they visited key areas in the world where there were major thinking skills projects in operation. Then, adopting an eclectic approach that embraced the most successful elements of the range of thinking skills programmes they had evaluated, they conducted an action research project with groups of disadvantaged learners and their teachers over an intensive period of ten years. Strategies and methodologies were trialled, evaluated and reflected upon by the researchers, the participating teachers, a group of educational psychologists and, importantly, the pupils. The key to the success of the action research lay in the quality of the reflection, consequent rethinking and trialling of the thinking skills and problem-solving strategies being used. This process culminated in the publication of *TASC: Thinking Actively in a Social Context* (Wallace and Adams 1993), which sets out a generic framework for the development of a thinking and problem-solving curriculum.

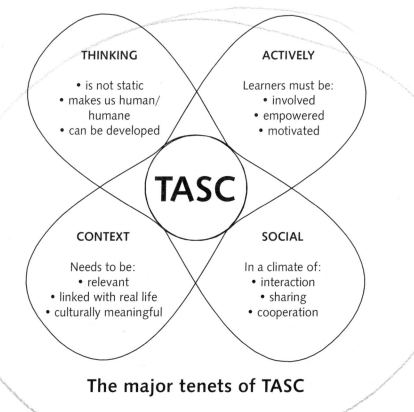

THINKING
• is not static
• makes us human/
  humane
• can be developed

ACTIVELY
Learners must be:
• involved
• empowered
• motivated

TASC

CONTEXT
Needs to be:
• relevant
• linked with real life
• culturally meaningful

SOCIAL
In a climate of:
• interaction
• sharing
• cooperation

The major tenets of TASC

Would you like to add any more ideas to the basic tenets of TASC?

REFLECT

PURPOSE   The remainder of this chapter examines the TASC framework: the theoretical base, the teaching methodology and the range of core skills and strategies that should be incorporated in any programme claiming to develop a problem-solving and thinking skills approach to the curriculum.

The subsequent chapters show TASC in action in primary schools:

- Chapter 2 shows how a primary school adopted a whole-school approach to the introduction of the TASC problem-solving and thinking skills. The staff and pupils agreed that they would work on the task of democratically establishing their school rules at the beginning of a new school year. (Currently the school is systematically working towards incorporating the range of problem-solving and thinking skills into the curriculum.)

- Chapters 3, 4 and 5 show how the TASC principles can be embedded in practice in selected areas of the literacy, numeracy and science National Curriculum Frameworks.

- Chapter 6 demonstrates how the TASC model can be used to develop a project through art and literacy. An additional purpose is to foster emotional intelligence and positive self-concept.

The purpose of the action research project that led to the development of TASC was to gather, trial and refine the most effective components of successful problem-solving strategies for both learners and teachers. The TASC model highlights essential elements that should be part of any thinking skills programme but it is not prescriptive with regard to its interpretation in the curriculum. The contributors to this text have brought their own expertise, experience, creativity and subject knowledge into the interpretation and application of TASC in action in the classroom.

Hence each contributor has interpreted the TASC problem-solving and thinking skills model in quite different ways, but the major tenets of TASC are clearly embedded throughout each chapter.

Understanding the theory that informs the base of TASC

COMMENT ▶   As professionals, we often make intuitive, 'feelings-based' decisions because we understand the needs of the children in our care: these are valid, diagnostic decisions, but we also need to be able to justify and defend those decisions with a backing of sound educational theory. Hence it is important to understand the two most important theories of how children best learn, which together form the underlying rationale from which TASC developed.

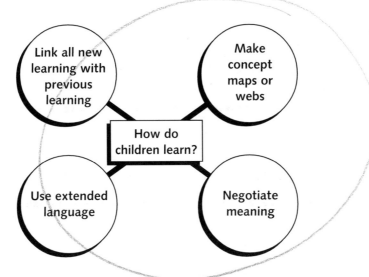

Vygotsky's 'Development of Higher Psychological Processes' (Wallace 2000)

Vygotsky (1978) stresses that children learn when they can make links with previous learning because then they can extend their existing conceptual mental map with new learning. Finding the mental 'hooks' within children's previous learning schemes is the creative art of a good teacher. The new learning 'transforms' the previous learning, creating new networks of understanding. Vygotsky discusses the essential role of the 'senior learner', who interacts with the young learner in order to negotiate meaning and understanding. The senior learner provides a scaffold of support until the apprentice, junior learner demonstrates competence and independence. The major tool for interaction is language, which first needs to be grounded within the child's informal language repertoire. Then the child's language can be gradually extended through understanding to accommodate the language for formal school learning. Also important are the role models children experience, for how else will they absorb patterns of behaviour? Responses, attitudes, emotions and thoughts are 'caught' rather than taught and while the home background of learners is fundamentally influential, the ethos, atmosphere and styles of behaviour within the classroom are also vitally important. Most importantly, Vygotsky argues that the processes of mediation and transformation are dynamic, making the learner always open to change and growth.

COMPONENTIAL

develop skills and strategies to plan, monitor, reflect and transfer

EXPERIENTIAL

deal with novelty, autonomise and transfer strategies

CONTEXTUAL

adapt, select and shape real-world environments

Sternberg's Triarchic Theory of Intellectual Development (Wallace 2000)

 **COMMENT** ▶ Robert Sternberg (1985) has led the way in rethinking the whole concept of the nature of 'intelligence' and of the processes by which children are enabled to learn more effectively. He maintains that even though our genetic inheritance varies and we are all individuals with different strengths and weaknesses, nevertheless we can all learn to use a range of thinking skills and strategies. These make up the components of our thinking processes, which derive from a repertoire of thinking tools that enable us to use our mental capacities more efficiently. We can all learn to plan and to monitor the efficiency of our planning. We can be taught how to reflect on our thinking processes in order to improve them and we can be assisted in the crystallisation of 'what' we know and 'how' we are learning. Then using our experiences and with mediated help, we can transfer the skills and strategies we learn to new situations and contexts. These are the key processes of metacognition: reflect, consolidate and transfer. Using our thinking and problem-solving skills, we adapt to our environment; and if we are lucky enough to have the opportunity, we select the environment in which we want to function. Possibly, the highest form of human endeavour is shown when we shape the environment around us: we become the 'movers' and the 'shakers' of the world we live in.

REFLECT ◖ Think about how you best learned:

● What kinds of thinking processes did you experience in school?

● What kinds of experiences consolidated your learning?

● Which skills have you retained as life skills and why did you retain them?

- What helped you to transfer your thinking skills from one context to another?

- What in real life has been your best learning experience?

- What do you think were the reasons for this?

- How much supposedly 'learned knowledge' have you forgotten?

- Which skills do you think are the most important for children to learn to use?

- Which teacher do you remember as your 'enabler'?

Considering the broad principles of the teaching methodology that underpins TASC

Outstanding teachers are 'gifted' in using both their awareness of themselves and their awareness of others to develop classroom rapport. As skilled communicators, they intuitively understand and respond effectively to the dynamics of the classroom. They are good mediators of learning, facilitators of interaction and often they become mentors who inspire children to learn.

PURPOSE

The purpose of this section is, therefore, not to suggest that the teaching principles of TASC are 'new' or 'revolutionary', but to invite you to reflect on, consolidate and confirm your good practice, and possibly extend your teaching strategies even further towards excellence.

The spiral diagram overleaf portrays the evolutionary nature of TASC teaching principles.

Use the spiral to do a reflective audit on your own classroom practice.

Write alongside the evolutionary stages in the spiral diagram the classroom practices you use to encourage the learners towards achieving competence in each stage of development.

Can you add any more ideas which in your experience lead towards successful practice?

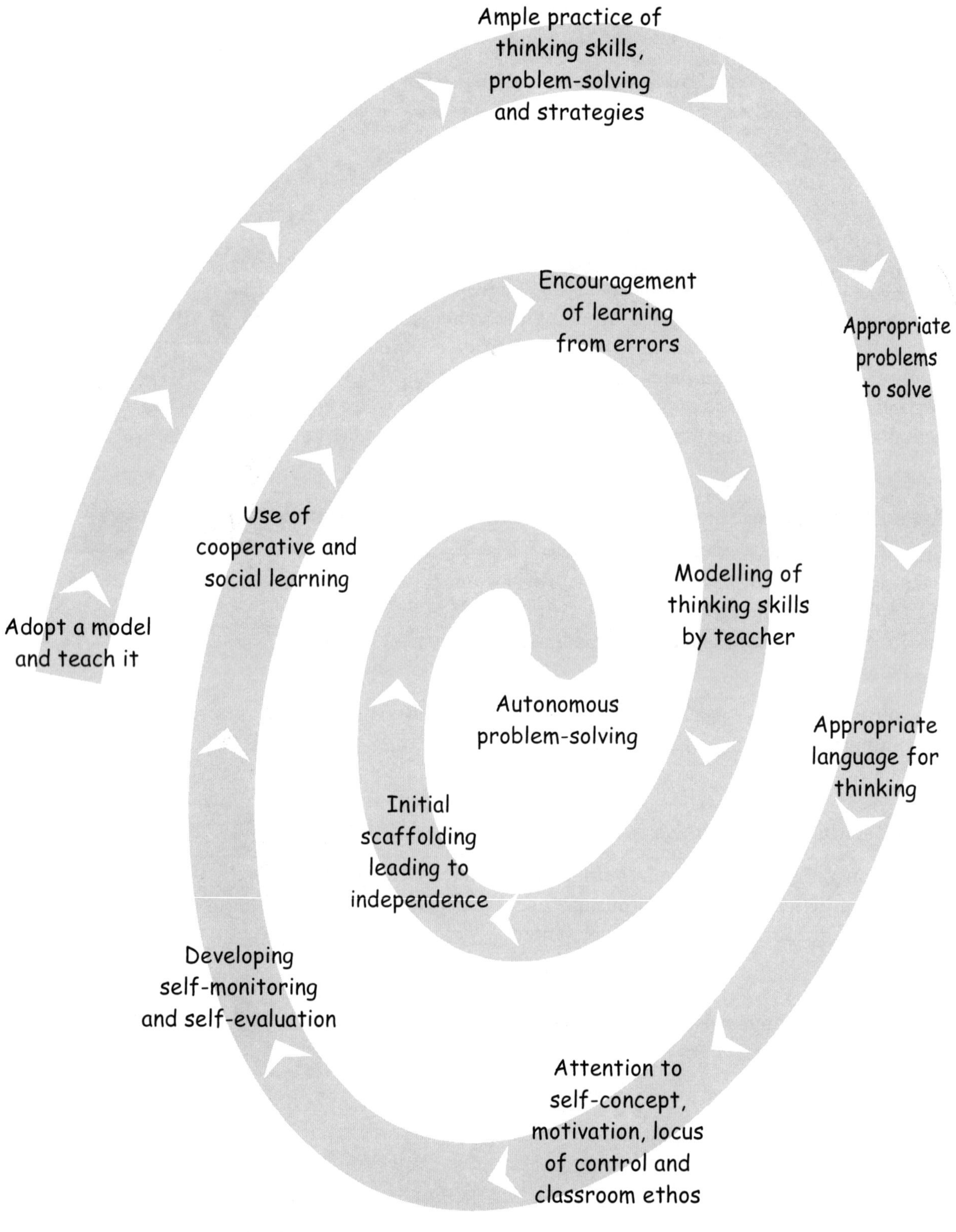

Ample practice of
thinking skills,
problem-solving
and strategies

Encouragement
of learning
from errors

Appropriate
problems
to solve

Use of
cooperative and
social learning

Modelling of
thinking skills
by teacher

Adopt a model
and teach it

Autonomous
problem-solving

Appropriate
language for
thinking

Initial
scaffolding
leading to
independence

Developing
self-monitoring
and self-evaluation

Attention to
self-concept,
motivation, locus
of control and
classroom ethos

Compare your reflective audit with the basic teaching principles that underpin TASC.

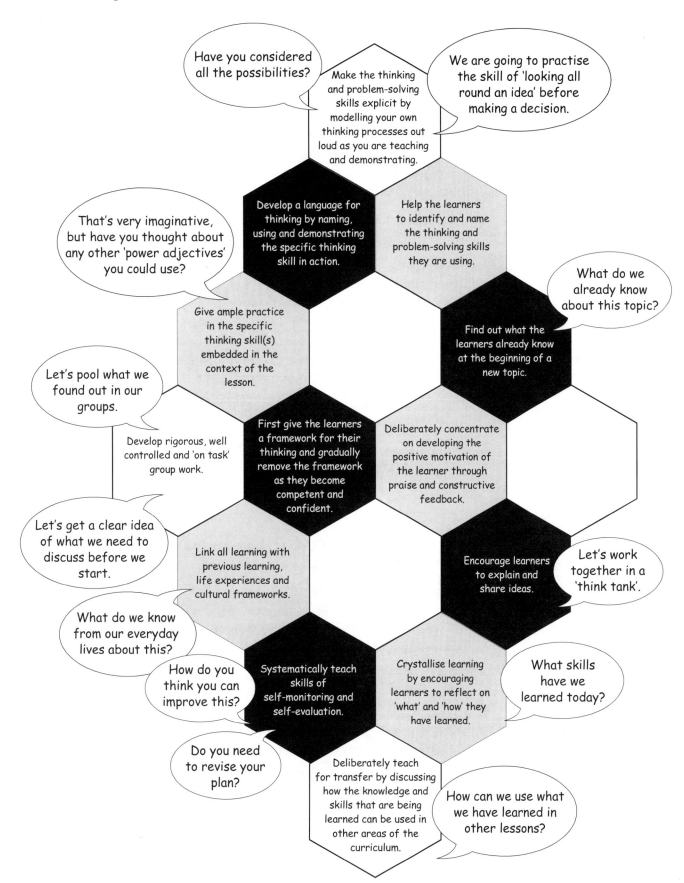

Putting the TASC problem-solving model and the teaching principles together in a menu of strategies for classroom use

COMMENT ▶

Every teacher has a repertoire of skills and strategies that are used appropriately for differing purposes. Working in a problem-solving and thinking skills way doesn't mean that we should never teach from the front, organise purposeful learning by rote, teach specific subject skills, give opportunities for necessary practice, show by demonstration or set individual work. However, teaching problem-solving and thinking skills within subjects and across the curriculum in a planned and coherent way actively develops learners' skills of learning how to learn and actively increases their mental capacities.

Always remember that any developmental change in our classroom practice takes time to consolidate!

Also, developing children's problem-solving and thinking skills *initially* takes time, but once children are familiar with the skills and using them, they learn more efficiently and we save time.

REFLECT ◀

Refer to the TASC problem-solving wheel on pages 14–15. Use it to reflect on your repertoire of classroom skills and strategies.

● Tick the strategies you use and give yourself a score from 5 (use regularly) to 1 (use occasionally).

● Think about the strategies you never use and consider how you can gradually incorporate these into your repertoire of teaching skills.

COMMENT ▶

While all the stages of the TASC problem-solving wheel are important, there are four critical stages:

● **Gather and organise** This stage is important because learners need to bring what they already know into their working memory ready for 'thinking, repair and extension'. This process also provides an excellent tool for assessing prior learning and enables the teacher to better differentiate the learning tasks that are set.

● **Identify** Many learners get lost and lose sight of the task they are undertaking, so it is important to clearly phrase the task using the learners' own words, as well as the criteria they will use to evaluate their work.

● **Evaluate** Pupils need training in the skill of evaluation, and they will need to discuss examples of 'good' and 'excellent' work that demonstrate the criteria they are working towards.

● **Learn from experience**   This is the final reflective stage when learners crystallise and consolidate what they have learned. It is vitally important that learners also reflect on the skills they have been using and how they might use these skills in other areas of the curriculum. This is the stage that is most often omitted because the lesson comes to an end and time has run out, and yet it is the most essential stage in bringing about retention of skills and transfer across the curriculum.

NOTE: A very good way to introduce the basic TASC problem-solving wheel is to use it to develop a practical problem-solving activity such as designing a new game, deciding on school rules or designing a new school (see Chapter 2).

Developing tools for effective thinking which feed into the TASC problem-solving wheel

In developing TASC, learners and teachers identified the tools for effective thinking that they used most often in the early stages of building their repertoire of thinking and problem-solving skills. It can be called a basic 'starter kit' and it is worth examining these core tools in detail.

COMMENT

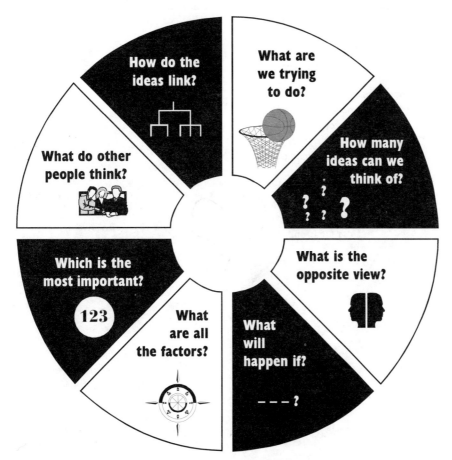

Some of the most commonly used TASC tools for effective thinking (Wallace 2000)

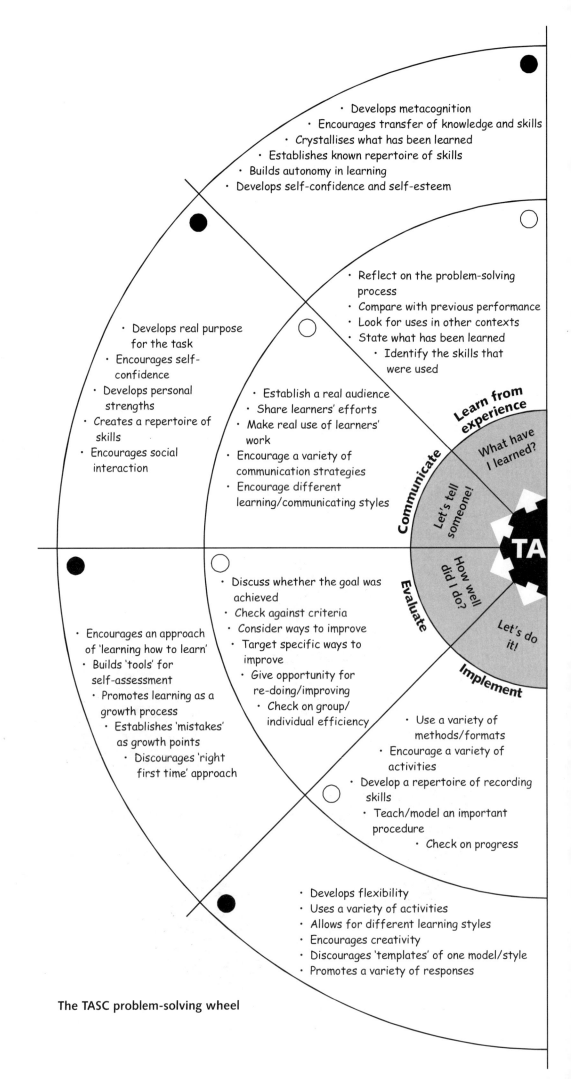

Develops metacognition
- Develops metacognition
- Encourages transfer of knowledge and skills
- Crystallises what has been learned
- Establishes known repertoire of skills
- Builds autonomy in learning
- Develops self-confidence and self-esteem

- Reflect on the problem-solving process
- Compare with previous performance
- Look for uses in other contexts
- State what has been learned
- Identify the skills that were used

- Develops real purpose for the task
- Encourages self-confidence
- Develops personal strengths
- Creates a repertoire of skills
- Encourages social interaction

- Establish a real audience
- Share learners' efforts
- Make real use of learners' work
- Encourage a variety of communication strategies
- Encourage different learning/communicating styles

Learn from experience
What have I learned?

Communicate
Let's tell someone!

Evaluate
How well did I do?

Let's do it!

Implement

TA

- Encourages an approach of 'learning how to learn'
- Builds 'tools' for self-assessment
- Promotes learning as a growth process
- Establishes 'mistakes' as growth points
- Discourages 'right first time' approach

- Discuss whether the goal was achieved
- Check against criteria
- Consider ways to improve
- Target specific ways to improve
- Give opportunity for re-doing/improving
- Check on group/individual efficiency

- Use a variety of methods/formats
- Encourage a variety of activities
- Develop a repertoire of recording skills
- Teach/model an important procedure
- Check on progress

- Develops flexibility
- Uses a variety of activities
- Allows for different learning styles
- Encourages creativity
- Discourages 'templates' of one model/style
- Promotes a variety of responses

The TASC problem-solving wheel

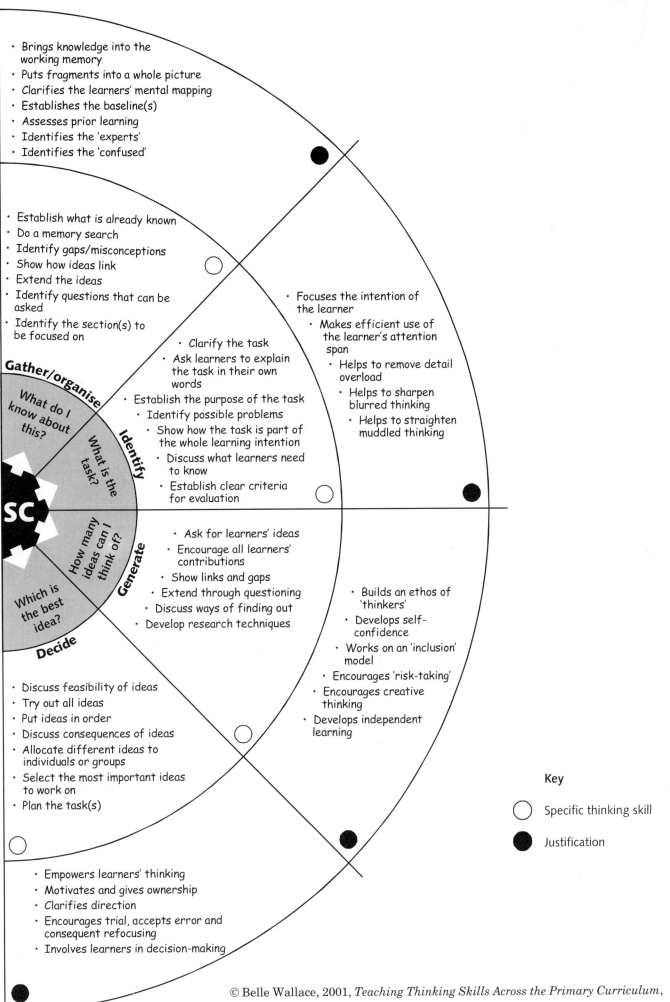

- Brings knowledge into the working memory
- Puts fragments into a whole picture
- Clarifies the learners' mental mapping
- Establishes the baseline(s)
- Assesses prior learning
- Identifies the 'experts'
- Identifies the 'confused'

- Establish what is already known
- Do a memory search
- Identify gaps/misconceptions
- Show how ideas link
- Extend the ideas
- Identify questions that can be asked
- Identify the section(s) to be focused on

Gather/organise

What do I know about this?

What is the task?

Identify

SC

- Clarify the task
- Ask learners to explain the task in their own words
- Establish the purpose of the task
- Identify possible problems
- Show how the task is part of the whole learning intention
- Discuss what learners need to know
- Establish clear criteria for evaluation

- Focuses the intention of the learner
- Makes efficient use of the learner's attention span
- Helps to remove detail overload
- Helps to sharpen blurred thinking
- Helps to straighten muddled thinking

How many ideas can I think of?

Generate

- Ask for learners' ideas
- Encourage all learners' contributions
- Show links and gaps
- Extend through questioning
- Discuss ways of finding out
- Develop research techniques

- Builds an ethos of 'thinkers'
- Develops self-confidence
- Works on an 'inclusion' model
- Encourages 'risk-taking'
- Encourages creative thinking
- Develops independent learning

Which is the best idea?

Decide

- Discuss feasibility of ideas
- Try out all ideas
- Put ideas in order
- Discuss consequences of ideas
- Allocate different ideas to individuals or groups
- Select the most important ideas to work on
- Plan the task(s)

- Empowers learners' thinking
- Motivates and gives ownership
- Clarifies direction
- Encourages trial, accepts error and consequent refocusing
- Involves learners in decision-making

Key

○ Specific thinking skill

● Justification

© Belle Wallace, 2001, *Teaching Thinking Skills Across the Primary Curriculum*, David Fulton Publishers.

Clarifying goals – What are we trying to do?

Many learners so easily go off track and get muddled or bogged down with what they are trying to do, often going round in circles and building up frustration and a sense of failure. So it is essential that learners constantly review and verbalise the purpose of their activity.

Creating a 'think-tank' – How many ideas can we think of?

There is seldom one right way to do something, or one worthwhile idea, and the creative thinker often sees the unusual way or has the unusual idea. When 'cascading' ideas it is important to work at speed for a few minutes only, to accept all ideas without comment and to encourage children to 'hitch-hike' on to each others' ideas.

Looking at both sides of an idea – What is the opposite view?

Stepping into someone else's shoes in any situation inevitably brings about a greater balance of opinion, decision or action. Getting learners to pause, role-play and review a perspective before accepting or acting on it means developing a mind pattern that helps to avoid an impulsive or biased viewpoint or action.

Exploring the consequences – What will happen if?

This is a tool for developing the imagination for considering alternatives, seeing possible consequences and questioning that which is normally accepted. It is the highly creative thinker who sees another way, changes the pattern or alters the usual and creates new knowledge.

Looking all round an idea – What are all the factors to consider?

Taking account of all the evidence, getting an overview of the whole situation before making a decision or planning a task, and preparing for possible contingencies enables learners to move more directly towards their goals. They are more thoroughly prepared and less likely to be diverted by factors they failed to consider.

Prioritising – Which is the most important?

Efficient learning behaviour stems from establishing which are the most important issues, ideas, stages or actions in any situation. Too often, learners waste time on less important tasks or fail to identify the essential points that lead to clear conclusions or the most efficient actions.

Consulting others – What do other people think?

Few people learn in isolation or invent something completely new. Most people benefit when they can consult others and compare viewpoints, theories, methods or styles. Sharing knowledge leads to greater understanding and cooperation.

Making the connections – How do the ideas link?

Every learner learns by making links with previous knowledge and extending those linkages in a way that makes sense. Making any kind of mindmap that connects ideas not only clarifies those ideas but allows the brain to take in information in an orderly way. Always organise the ideas from a cascade in some way, e.g. prioritise them or group them for a specific purpose.

Think about the core tools for effective thinking outlined above.

- Are there any other tools for effective thinking that you often use?

- Can you give practical examples of when you have used any of the core tools? How successful were they? What might you change if you repeated them?

Extending the TASC tools for effective thinking

There are many thinking strategies that can be called tools for effective thinking. Some of these are subject specific, while others are used across the curriculum. The following mindmap (p. 18) gives a comprehensive overview of a wide range of cross-curricular thinking tools. The mindmap is useful as a checklist when planning classroom activities. Most of the tools are both necessary and suitable for all learners although the language would need to be adjusted to suit their levels of understanding. Some of the tools are particularly suitable for the more able learners who show that they are ready for more challenging activities to extend their thinking to higher levels.

When learners understand the process of the thinking they are practising, it is important to give the thinking tool a name so that the learners are acquiring a thinking skills vocabulary.

You can use this mindmap as a checklist for your long-term planning. It is important to steadily and consistently incorporate the thinking vocabulary into your lessons.

REFLECT

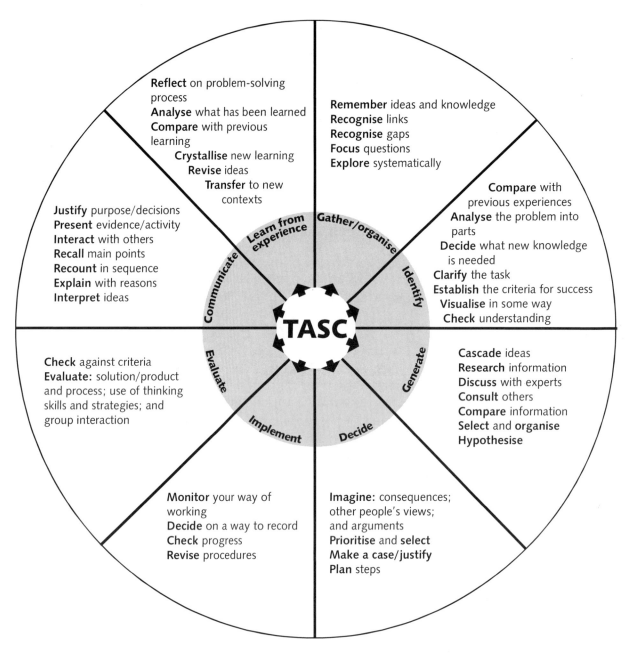

Reflect on problem-solving process
Analyse what has been learned
Compare with previous learning
Crystallise new learning
Revise ideas
Transfer to new contexts

Remember ideas and knowledge
Recognise links
Recognise gaps
Focus questions
Explore systematically

Justify purpose/decisions
Present evidence/activity
Interact with others
Recall main points
Recount in sequence
Explain with reasons
Interpret ideas

Compare with previous experiences
Analyse the problem into parts
Decide what new knowledge is needed
Clarify the task
Establish the criteria for success
Visualise in some way
Check understanding

Check against criteria
Evaluate: solution/product and process; use of thinking skills and strategies; and group interaction

Cascade ideas
Research information
Discuss with experts
Consult others
Compare information
Select and **organise**
Hypothesise

Monitor your way of working
Decide on a way to record
Check progress
Revise procedures

Imagine: consequences; other people's views; and arguments
Prioritise and **select**
Make a case/justify
Plan steps

Learn from experience · Gather/organise · Communicate · **TASC** · Identify · Evaluate · Generate · Implement · Decide

Extending the TASC tools for effective thinking

Extending children's questioning for thinking

Children need to develop a range of self-questioning techniques that they learn to use automatically when they are working on an individual task or on a cooperative task. In order to develop the children's repertoire, it is necessary that we model the questions whenever it is possible to do so. The following mindmap gives suggestions of questions that can be used at each stage of the TASC problem-solving wheel. Of course, the list is not comprehensive and many more possible questions can be added.

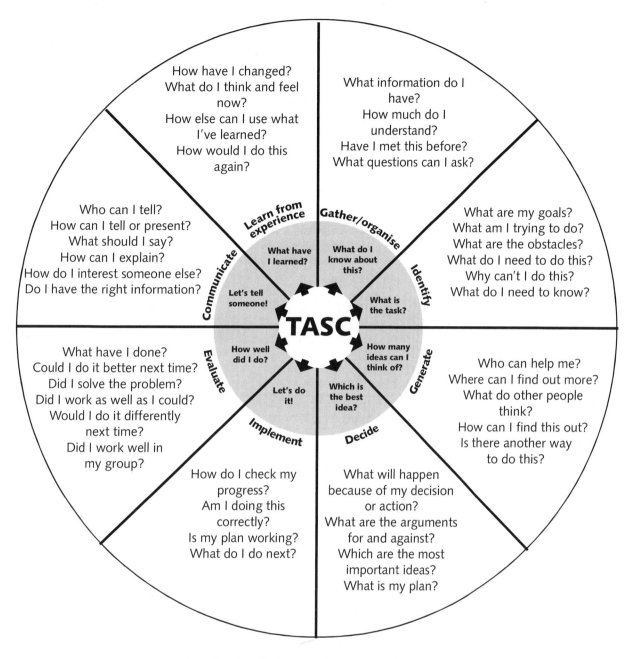

Questions to develop thinking in the TASC problem-solving model

Once again, take time to do a reflective audit of the questions which are a natural pattern in your teaching repertoire. If necessary, make a conscious effort to widen the range of questions you use in the classroom.

Conclusion

Why TASC: thinking actively in a social context?

There is a worldwide plea for school curricula that develop learners who are thinkers and problem-solvers so that solutions to the ever increasing complexities that trouble people's personal and public lives can be found. But, apart from that need, thinking is what makes us human and humane, caring and responsible, creative and alive.

However, thinking derives from our life experiences in which we are actively engaged; from our imaginations, which fire creativity and action; from the real problems that we need to overcome. Too often, thinking skills programmes have been 'add-ons', tagged on in special classes purporting to develop thinkers. This sticking plaster approach seldom, if ever, results in developing individuals who are active thinkers. For learners to become active lifelong thinkers, the skills and strategies they need to use must be actively embedded in the curriculum, in real-life problems, in relevant contexts.

Although a few people prefer to work in isolation, most people thrive when they can exchange ideas, talk a problem through with another person, cooperate in an endeavour, discuss possibilities and extend their own thinking through interaction. We are essentially social beings and need to communicate with others. But we also need to practise the skills of democratic behaviour through repeated classroom experiences of working cooperatively with others.

We learn best when we:

- understand the relevance of our learning;

- can relate to the cultural context;

- can appreciate the significance of the tasks that are set;

- can see the purpose of the fragments as part of the whole picture;

- feel that we are capable of learning;

- develop more complex mental schemes that are extensions of what we already know;

- can hook into new knowledge from the base we have already;

- acquire new techniques and thinking skills through modelling and demonstration;

- try out skills for ourselves until we gain the competence and confidence to be independent.

Developing learners' problem-solving and thinking skills is an essential ingredient in the development of a humane and empowering curriculum that conveys the school ethos that all learners are valuable and capable. As educators, we are already making a great effort to do a good job, but we can extend our professional practice even more, gradually and systematically, until we are professionals with excellence.

My TASC problem-solving wheel

Pupils can cut out and laminate their TASC problem-solving wheels then fasten them with paper-fasteners into an exercise book or thinking skills log book. Or the pupils can redesign the wheels and invent their own symbols for each stage of problem-solving. Then pupils can use the wheels to guide their thinking and planning. It is a good idea to ask the pupils to keep a portfolio of their best work, which demonstrates the range of thinking tools they have used. It is also very important that all the skills are developed across the curriculum.

A very good way to introduce TASC is through a practical activity such as: designing a new game, deciding on school rules or planning a new school.

Some of my TASC tools for effective thinking

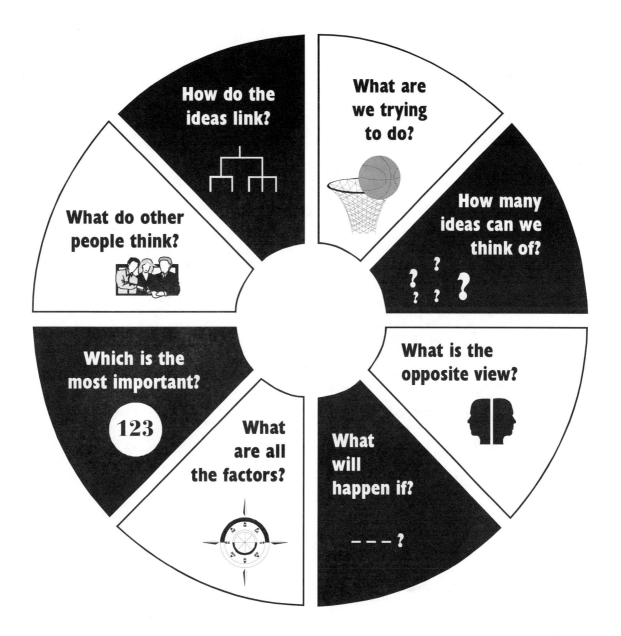

Pupils can also draw an additional outer ring around this wheel and then they can record how they used the tools for effective thinking in a particular project.

Title: _____

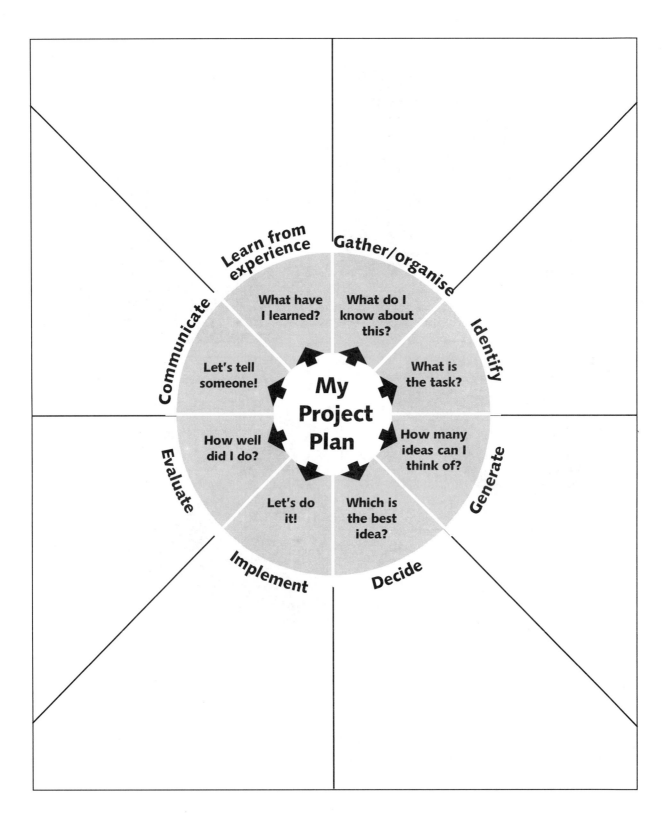

You can enlarge this activity sheet and pupils can use it to plan and record the stages of their thinking and problem-solving. It is a good idea for pupils to keep their activity record sheets in a thinking-skills log book or in a portfolio of their best work.

Questions to develop my thinking in TASC problem-solving

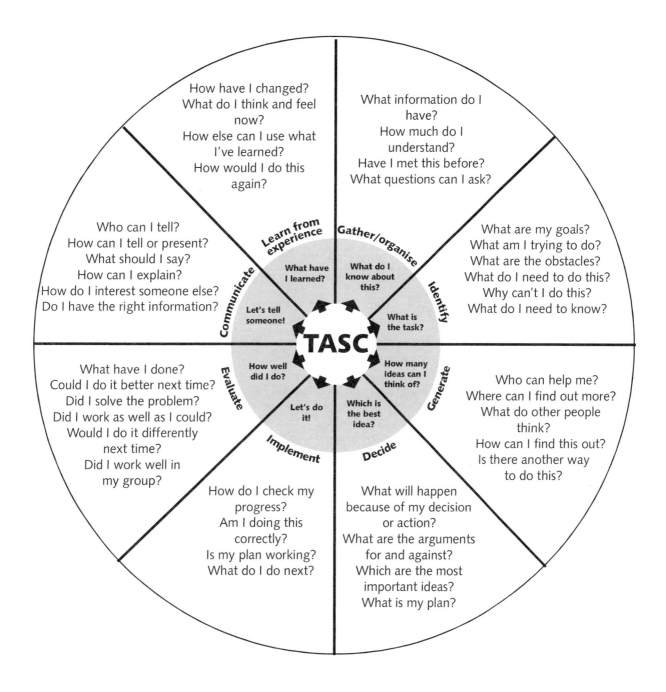

Introducing TASC Across a Whole Key Stage – a Case Study

DIANA CAVE

We are all children of our environment – the good no less than the bad, – products of that particular group of habits, customs, traditions, ways of looking at things, standards of right and wrong, which chance has presented to our still growing and expanding consciousness.

Emily Lawless, *Hurrish* (1886)

Introduction

A very effective and holistic way to introduce the TASC approach to problem-solving and thinking skills is to embed the thinking processes and teaching methodology in a real and relevant problem for a class, a Key Stage or even a whole school. Then the children can be actively working to an end product that is tangible and useful: they can be guided to use a planned problem-solving approach and to reflect on how efficiently they worked and which thinking skills they used. Some examples of problems are: redesigning the school playground, organising a school disco, organising a concert for senior citizens, producing a school magazine and solving a litter problem. However, the skills used in the real problem-solving exercise then need to be systematically embedded in the curriculum.

COMMENT

Note: The TASC project was carried out at the National School, Lincs.

PURPOSE

The purpose of this chapter is to share the experience of one school that decided to introduce the TASC problem-solving strategy to children throughout the school as the initial target at the beginning of a new school year. As a school, we believed it would benefit all children, by providing structured independence to the most able and valuable scaffolding to those children in need of support and guidance.

Background information

Our school has 480 Key Stage 2 children grouped into 16 mixed ability classes, four per year group.

The TASC approach had been explored during in-service education and training (INSET) for the whole staff, and small pilot studies with groups of able children had been trialled in Years 4 to 6 during the spring term.

During the summer term, the school's curriculum coordinator undertook a further INSET course, investigating classroom extension activities for the more able in Years 5 and 6. It was then decided as a staff development initiative to implement the TASC approach to developing problem-solving and thinking skills across the curriculum.

Devising a timetable

We felt it was important to give the children a thorough grounding in the TASC strategy from the very beginning. Our school, like all schools, runs on a very tight timetable, which is further compounded by the complexities of 'setting' in English and mathematics. To this end, we set aside the opening four days of the school year as a TASC week. This enabled us to lay the foundations for cooperative working and to establish the elements of the TASC wheel. This introductory period was then followed by sessions, over the course of a year (Figure 2.1), in which individual subject areas were connected to the TASC wheel.

Preparing for the TASC week

At the end of the summer term, staff were given lesson planning sheets, a TASC week timetable (Figure 2.2) and an information sheet listing items that needed to be collected (Figure 2.3). Year groups were split to ease pressure on design and technology (D&T) resources at the end of the week. Timetable demands prohibited the overflow of activities into the following week.

Five lessons provided the backbone of introducing TASC throughout the school. They were of varying length, ranging from one hour to a whole day. Each day was preceded by input from the curriculum coordinator, taking the staff through the lesson plans, pointing out possi-

September/October (4 days, 6 weeks)				November/December (7 weeks, 3 days)		
First four days Introduce TASC wheel: • class rules • promoting a new product	**Week 2** Use TASC wheel in **science** investigations	TASC **numeracy** investigation	HALF TERM	Construct TASC tools chart, and display it alongisde the TASC wheel	**Final full week** literacy project/ TASC approach	TASC **numeracy** investigation

January/February (3 days, 6 weeks)			November/December (7 weeks, 3 days)
Use TASC in **literacy** when practical, and in half-termly **numeracy** investigations	HALF TERM		TASC – literacy and numeracy
TASC – **science**			TASC – **science**

April/May (5 weeks)			June/July (7 weeks)
Extend TASC approach to **remaining subjects** when appropriate	HALF TERM		Use TASC across the **whole curriculum** in appropriate lessons
literacy and **numeracy**			Staff review of TASC in the curriculum. Introduce a TASC log book for use in the next year
TASC – **science**			Research, recording and communication skills

Figure 2.1   Developing thinking and problem-solving skills – a proposed calendar

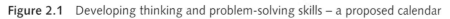

Years 4 & 6	Tuesday	Wednesday	Thursday	Friday
Morning	Rules for group talk	Introduce TASC wheel	Produce product to promote TASC	
Afternoon	Negotiate and agree class rules	Design TASC product		

Years 3 & 5	Tuesday	Wednesday	Thursday	Friday
Morning			Introduce TASC wheel	Produce product to promote TASC
Afternoon	Rules for group talk	Negotiate and agree class rules	Design TASC product	

Figure 2.2   The TASC week timetable

Preparation by the class teacher	Activities	End product
Collect samples of a variety of promotional items to advertise a new product. Look for: • **claims** truthful / exaggerated • **visual tactics** for grabbing attention • **linguistic devices**: puns, jingles, alliteration, invented words These will be needed during the **first week of term**.	Establish rules for group talk (1 hr). Establish class rules (1 hr). Establish TASC process used in agreeing class rules (2 hrs). Promoting TASC: Planning – 2 hrs Making – whole day	Rules for group talk displayed in each classroom. Classroom rules displayed in each classroom and a copy sent to JG. TASC wheel displayed in each classroom. (You will have the basis of a display, but will need to apply finishing techniques to your product.) Display of products in the hall – to be viewed by each class, photographed, then returned to classrooms for use.

Figure 2.3 Staff information sheet

ble pitfalls, distributing recording sheets and so on. Staff were asked to record all discussions on sheets of A1 paper so that these could later be used for reflection of the thinking and problem-solving processes that had been used. These meetings also provided the opportunity to revise knowledge and understanding of the TASC wheel with staff who had not been directly involved in the pilot study and of informing and supporting staff for whom TASC was completely new.

Laying the groundwork – focusing on cooperative interaction: establishing the rules of group talk

Lesson plan 1

The first focused lesson of TASC week required the children to talk effectively in order to agree a set of rules for group talk. The concept of 'rules' was discussed as a class. We talked at length about what rules are, where we find rules and why we have rules. We considered the way in which we speak and listen in a class group: taking turns in speaking, connecting contributions to what has gone before, taking different views into account, extending ideas in the light of discussion, giving reasons for opinions.

While keeping in mind the conditions necessary for successful group talk, each group of 4–6 pupils was given a plastic drinks bottle and asked to generate as many ideas for its use as possible. Ideas came thick and fast and involved even the more timid children. After five minutes each group was asked to single out the most interesting idea. Much debate ensued and eventually each group was prepared to report back to the class. This activity was very important because the children needed a practical activity in which they were interacting as a group, so that they could reflect on their *actions* rather than just talking hypothetically about them.

Following discussion of the weird and wonderful things that a plastic bottle could be used for, we turned our attention once more to the rules of group talk. We reflected on episodes of both productive and restrictive exchange of ideas, listing observations as we proceeded. We considered the willingness to participate, to take turns, to listen to the views of others, to build on the suggestions of others, to justify statements, to deal politely with opposing views and to adopt key roles within the discussion.

Next, we deliberated on how we could improve the quality of group talk in the future. This focused mainly on the appointment of key roles (scribe, spokesperson, chairperson) and of maintaining respect for those with a particular position. A set of group discussion rules was drafted, discussed and amended until we arrived at a set with which everyone was in agreement.

In the plenary we read through the rules together and reflected on how well we had achieved our aims. It was concluded that, with our new set of rules, future group talks would be even more effective.

Agreeing a set of class rules – using a 'veiled' TASC strategy

Lesson plan 2

The objectives of this lesson were: to talk effectively as members of a group; to agree a set of class rules; to use all stages of the TASC wheel. However, we did not wish to complicate the issue of agreeing class rules – something that we undertake as a school each September – so we made the decision to guide the children through the processes of the TASC wheel without initially drawing their attention directly to it. We would draw out the stages of the TASC wheel during the vital stage of reflecting on 'what' and 'how' we had learned. The work in this lesson was done on A3 paper and post-it notes and kept as reference for the subsequent lesson.

The illustrations on the following pages were drawn by the children when they began to transfer the TASC thinking skills into their classroom lesson work.

Children's TASC wheel work 1: Gather and organise

The introductory discussion provided the opportunity to gather and organise, to deliberate on 'What do I already know about this?' We recapped on the purpose of rules, on the rules of their previous class and on the intended audience for our rules: children, teachers, assistants, caretaker, etc. We also considered the phrasing of rules, feeling that we responded rather more agreeably to a polite notice – 'Thank you for taking your litter home' – than to a more abrupt one – 'Keep Off'.

Gather and organise

Children's TASC wheel work 2: Identify

Identifying the task was the second step. We were clear in our purpose – we wanted a set of class rules that would generate the best possible learning environment.

In groups of 4–6 the children reviewed their newly formed 'Rules of group talk' and appointed a chairperson and a scribe/spokesperson.

Identify

Children's TASC wheel work 3: Generate

The groups were asked to generate ideas for classroom rules, writing each idea on a separate post-it note.

Generate

Recording an idea for a classroom rule

Children's TASC wheel work 4: Decide

The next act was to decide on the relative importance of the ideas. Much sticking and rearranging accompanied intense discussion as the children debated the priority of rules.

Decide

I think this one goes next because . . .

Children's TASC wheel work 5: Implement

The time had come to implement our findings. Taking just the three most important rules, each group discussed, amended and enlarged the wording for display. Some rules became much more precise, some remained unchanged and others became broader to incorporate 'lost' rules from further down the priority list.

Implement

The spokespersons presented their groups' ideas, blu-tacking them to the whiteboard. Similar thoughts were automatically grouped together.

The suggestions were discussed and subdivided into three groups – 'definite rules', 'possible rules' and 'unnecessary rules'. The wording of the 'definite rules' was discussed and agreed and incorporated several of the 'possible rules'.

Children's TASC wheel work 6: Evaluate

We read our new classroom rules and evaluated how well we had done. We felt pleased with our efforts – the rules considered everyone who entered our classroom; they were manageable; they were fair and everyone agreed to try to keep to them.

Evaluate

Children's TASC wheel work 7: Communicate

It was time to communicate the rules to others. The computer was ready and within a few minutes we had a copy for pinning inside the door, the first thing visitors to our room would see, and a second copy to send to the head teacher.

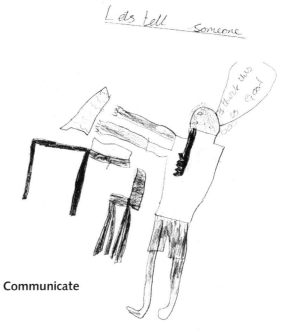

Communicate

Children's TASC wheel work 8: Learn from experience

The plenary focused attention on learning from experience. We reflected on what we had learned, how well we had contributed ideas and how we had interacted with others.

Learn from experience

Introducing the TASC wheel

Lesson plan 3

The purpose of this lesson was to reflect on the activities in Lessons 1 and 2, and to unveil and clearly identify the TASC stages used in the previous sessions.

The introduction focused on how athletes and sporting personalities prepare for major competitions, training the whole body and not just individual parts. This was followed by an explanation that we can train our brains to be more efficient and effective thinkers and problem-solvers.

On the wall we had a large circle, divided equally into eight segments. In readiness were the TASC segment labels.

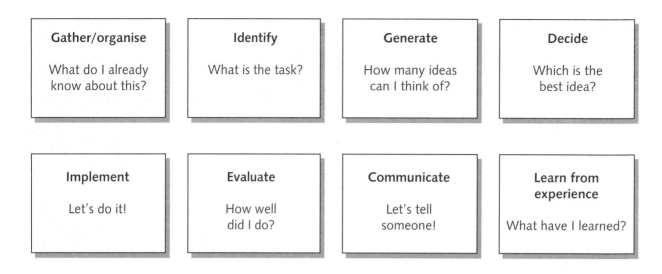

Gather/organise	**Identify**	**Generate**	**Decide**
What do I already know about this?	What is the task?	How many ideas can I think of?	Which is the best idea?

Implement	**Evaluate**	**Communicate**	**Learn from experience**
Let's do it!	How well did I do?	Let's tell someone!	What have I learned?

We read the 'Gather/organise' label together. This was followed by the explanation and discussion:

Do you remember yesterday when we brainstormed ideas about rules? What we were doing was gathering and organising our thoughts. We were answering the question 'What do I already know about this?'

So that's what we were doing!

At this point, the label and yesterday's Sheet 1 (the initial brainstorm about rules – reduced to A4 on the photocopier) were positioned in the first segment of the wheel.

The remainder of the wheel was built up in the same fashion – reading the label, referring back to the previous session's activity, discussing what we did and why we did it, then placing the appropriate label and A4 copy of the recording sheet on to the wheel. From time to time we stopped to review progress from the beginning. The construction of the wheel progressed very naturally; the children quickly realised what the next step was and contributed eagerly.

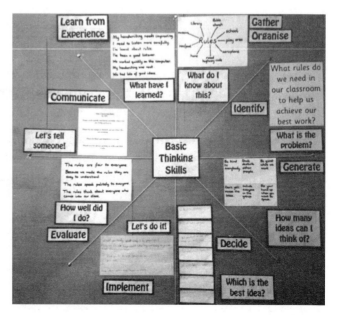

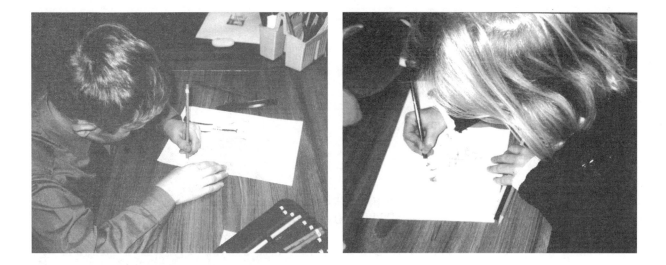

The completed wheel was introduced to the children as the TASC wheel and an explanation of the initials TASC was given.

At this point, children were encouraged to produce their own individual TASC wheels, illustrating each segment with an image representative of each particular part of the wheel. Other children worked in groups of eight, each taking one segment of a larger TASC wheel to interpret.

As consolidation, the plenary focused on the fact that we can train our brains to work better and that we would be using the TASC wheel as a way of doing just that.

Design and make a promotional TASC product

Lesson plan 4

This lesson was spread over two days: designing on Day 1 and producing the finished product on Day 2.

We began by reviewing the TASC process and its intended purpose. We identified the need to tell people about our new-found approach to thinking and problem-solving. Like any new product on the market, it needed advertising. We discussed the ways in which new products are drawn to our attention: through TV and newspaper adverts, radio jingles, product displays, give-aways and so on. Next we explored the tricks of the trade, including claims, visual tactics and linguistic devices. The children brainstormed ideas for slogans (Figure 2.4).

Establishing the children as the consumers of this new product was an important and necessary step. We acknowledged the interest of other parties – parents, support assistants, etc. – but viewed pupils as the primary target group.

The children worked in pairs or small groups to generate a vast array of ideas for promotional products. They then focused their attention on a single idea, which they explained to the class.

Figure 2.4 Generating TASC slogans

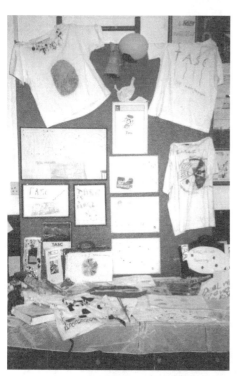

Each child produced an equipment/materials list and identified the sequence of necessary activities involved.

The production day began with a review of the purpose and audience for the products and a reminder about using equipment safely. Then the children implemented their plans.

The intended products involved the use of toolboxes, electrical components, construction kits, paint, needlework, clay, computers, tape recorders, video cameras and musical instruments.

Evaluation was conducted as the work progressed: around the table with peers, with the class teacher, with adults moving around the school and on the playground. Products were tested and improved throughout the day. Most items were completed within the time available; a few were finished off in subsequent lunchtimes. We reflected on the success of the designing and making activities, on the skills we have, on those we need to develop and on the cooperative interaction with others.

The following week a whole-school display was mounted. The children eagerly spotted their own products and admired those made by others. Lots of excited discussion was heard along the lines of 'Next time, I'm going to . . .'

REFLECT

The TASC week passed quickly and productively. The advanced planning, the pre-lesson information sessions and the post-lesson discussions gave everyone a sense of real purpose and a stress-free start to the new school year. The children were excited and focused on what they were asked to do. Working together in this way, as a whole school, was something of a novelty for us as we are usually very rigidly timetabled – ideas, resources and expertise were shared and year group divisions disappeared as we undertook a common, unifying task.

Having established TASC as a basic thinking and problem-solving concept we are now preparing to extend the approach across the whole curriculum.

Lesson Plan 1

Date:	Curriculum area: English – Speaking and listening	Cross-curricular/ PSHE links
POS 3a–e	**Learning objectives:** • to talk effectively to members of a group • to agree a set of rules for group talk	PSHE 1, 2, 4 Developing confidence and responsibility.

Introduction

Class discussion: What are rules?   Where do we have rules?
Why do we have rules?   List all ideas.

Preparing to play an active role as citizens.

Activity

Explanation: We are going to discuss a question in groups and report our ideas to the other groups.

Consider the rules you might need to hold a successful group discussion. List all ideas.

Give a plastic bottle, a sheet of paper and a pen or pencil to each group of 4–6 children.

Developing good relationships and respecting the differences between people.

Vocabulary
Chair(person)
Scribe
Spokesperson

Challenge: Thinking about the suggested rules for group talk:
a in the next five minutes, generate as many ideas as possible for the possible uses of a plastic bottle
b take ten minutes to discuss the ideas and decide on the most interesting or unusual idea
c report back to the rest of the class and discuss your ideas with them.
Vote on the best idea.

Differentiation
Grouping: mixed ability; the less confident supported by the presence of a friend.

Main focus: Reflect on the success or otherwise of each group's discussion. List observations.

Support

Consider participation by individuals within the group: willingness to take turns (dominant/bossy, shy/reluctant); listening to each other's ideas; justifying statements; dealing politely with opposing points of view; taking up and sustaining different roles, such as chair, scribe and spokesman.

Resources
Plastic bottles
Pens and pencils
Paper

Consider how we can improve the quality of group discussions in the future: establishing roles; respecting the role of chair; listening carefully; asking questions; involving everyone.

Key Assessment

Draft, discuss, amend and agree a set of group discussion rules.

Plenary

Read through the set of group discussion rules together.

Reflect: Have **we** done a good job?   How well did **I** work?

Notes/implications for future planning

Produce a 'Group discussion rules' poster for the classroom.

Produce a set of 'Group discussion rules' sheets for use in future group discussion.

Lesson Plan 2

Date:	Curriculum area: English – Speaking and listening	Cross-curricular/ PSHE links
POS 3a–e	**Learning objectives:** • to talk effectively to members of a group • to agree a set of class rules • to use all stages of the TASC wheel	PSHE 1, 2, 4 Developing confidence and responsibility.

## Introduction **Keep all sheets for tomorrow** **Gather:** What do I already know about this? **Class discussion:** Purpose of rules and rules of group discussion. 　　　　　　　Consider everyone: children, caretaker, support assistants, teachers. 　　　　　　　Phrasing: Keep Out! Thank you for taking your litter home.		Preparing to play an active role as citizens. Developing good relationships and respecting the differences between people.

Activity

Identify: What is the task?
Explanation: We have been hearing about our school Code of Conduct in assembly. We are going to work in groups to discuss ideas for our class rules and report our ideas to the other groups.
Organise groups. Have the children appoint a chair, scribe/spokesperson.
Think about the environment in which you could work most effectively.

Generate: How many ideas can I think of?
a In the next 10 minutes, generate as many ideas as possible for our classroom rules. Write just one idea on a post-it note.

Decide: Which is the best idea?
b Now you have 15 minutes to discuss each idea, put them in order of importance, stick them on to the long orange strip of paper and finally number each note.

Implement: Let's do it!
c Spend 5–10 minutes discussing the wording of the three most important rules. Write these three rules clearly on yellow strips of paper.
d Have the spokespersons report back, reading one rule at a time and displaying them for everyone to see. (Use blu-tack, because they will be moved around.)
e Have the children organise ideas by grouping similar ideas together.
f Discuss the suggestions as a class. Order the rules in terms of importance.
g Vote on which rules are wanted. Agree on the wording, keeping the rules as positive as possible. Write the agreed rules.

Evaluate: How well did I do?
Examine the completed rules. Have we done a good job? Are we pleased with our efforts? Why?
Consider how well the discussion process was conducted.
Did everyone abide by the group discussion rules? How could it have been improved?

Communicate: Let's tell someone!
Appoint two children to print two copies of the class rules: for the classroom and JG.

Vocabulary
Chair(person)
Scribe
Spokesperson

Differentiation
Grouping: mixed ability; the less confident supported by the presence of a friend.

Support

Resources
Post-it notes
Pens/pencils
A3 paper
Paper strips
Blu-tack
Computer

Key Assessment

Plenary

Learn from experience: What have I learned?
Encourage children to reflect on and discuss their own contribution and their interaction with others.

Notes/implications for future planning

Lesson Plan 3

Date:

Curriculum area: English – Speaking and listening

POS 3a–e

Learning objectives:

- to introduce/reintroduce the TASC wheel to children
- to show how we have already used all the stages of the TASC wheel

Introduction

Discussion: How do athletes prepare for the Olympic Games? Develop the idea of training the whole body and not just one part of it. Explain that we can train our brains to be more efficient/effective thinkers and problem-solvers.

Activity

Introduce/reintroduce the TASC wheel.
Years 5 and 6: Establish prior knowledge by brainstorming and recording ideas.
All years: Read through the TASC wheel headings one at a time.

Gather/organise: What do I already know about this?
Do you remember yesterday when we brainstormed our ideas about rules? Show yesterday's Sheet 1. What we were doing was gathering and organising our thoughts/knowledge. We were answering the question 'What do I already know about this?' Attach the label provided and display.

Identify: What is the task?
The second activity yesterday was to identify the problem/task. We need to be certain about what we are trying to achieve whenever we begin something. The problem/task yesterday was to agree a set of class rules. Show Sheet 2. Attach the label provided and display.

Generate: How many ideas can I think of?
Show a blank sheet, Sheet 3. What did we do on this sheet with all these boxes? We wrote down all the ideas we could think of. Add a few sample suggestions. Attach the label provided and display.

Decide: Which is the best idea?
You had lots of ideas. What was the next step? We had to decide 'Which is the best idea?' We blu-tacked them to the orange strips of paper in order of importance. Attach the label provided and display.

Implement: Let's do it!
Now we were ready to accomplish the task: to agree a set of class rules. Can you recall what we did next? We collected yellow strips; grouped similar ideas together; arranged the rules in order of importance; decided which to keep; and agreed wording. Attach the label provided to Sheet 5 and display.

Evaluate: How well did I do?
When we complete a task it is important to evaluate the end product. Yesterday we looked at our completed rules and thought about how successful we had been. Show Sheet 6. This is what we thought about how well we did. Attach the label provided and display.

Communicate: Let's tell someone!
Once we were happy with the result of our efforts it was important to tell someone. We communicated/shared our work with the head teacher. Attach the class rules to the labelled sheet and display.

Learn from experience: What have I learned?
Finally, we reflected on our own performance. We thought about what we had learned, not just in terms of knowledge but in terms of our contribution and interaction with others. Attach the label provided to Sheet 8 and display.

Examine the completed wheel. This is called the **TASC wheel**. Improve the TASC wheel, refining a classroom wheel for reference and individual TASC memos if time is available.

Plenary

Consolidation: We can train our brains to be more efficient/effective thinkers and problem-solvers. We are going to use the TASC wheel to help train our brains.

Notes/implications for future planning

Cross-curricular/ PSHE links
PSHE 1, 2, 4
Developing confidence and responsibility.

Preparing to play an active role as citizens.

Developing good relationships and respecting the differences between people.

Vocabulary
Gather
Organise
Identify
Generate
Decide
Implement
Evaluate
Communicate
Reflect

Differentiation

Support

Resources
Ideas recorded yesterday
Display labels and sheets
Blu-tack

Key Assessment

Lesson Plan 4

Date:	Curriculum area: Design and technology	Cross-curricular/ PSHE links
POS 3a–e	**Learning objectives:** • to design, produce and evaluate products to promote implementation of the TASC model	**English** 1 Composition 2 Planning/ drafting 5 Handwriting and presentation

Introduction

Discussion: **Gather/organise:** recall information about the TASC process and its purpose.
Identify the task: TASC is new to most of the school. Like any new product, it needs to be advertised.

Activity

Generate: How many ideas can I think of?

- Discuss ways in which new goods are promoted, including: claims – truthful/exaggerated; visual tactics for grabbing attention; linguistic devices – puns, jingles, alliteration, invented words.
- Look at advertising phrases – Beans means Heinz, etc.
- Brainstorm class ideas: TASC – Learning to Learn; TASC – STRETCHING your Mind; TASC for Brain Training, etc.
- Establish that the children will be the users/consumers of the new product and the purpose of TASC.

Working in pairs or small groups, generate ideas for promotional products (advertisements, leaflets, flags, posters, badges, bookmarks, T-shirts, video adverts, musical jingles, banners, jigsaws, pencil cases, pencil pots/holders, fridge magnets, rotating or illuminated signs, and so on).

Decide: Which is the best idea?

Select, develop and explain the preferred idea. Plan what equipment, materials and components are needed and identify the sequence of actions.

The following day – after assembling the necessary equipment and material

Reminder: audience, purpose, safety, etc.

Implement: Let's do it!

Discuss the plan with the teacher. Assemble equipment, materials and components. Create the product, suggesting alternative ways of continuing if the first attempts fail. Use finishing techniques to strengthen and improve the appearance of the product, using a range of equipment, including ICT.

Evaluate: How well did I do?

Encourage the children to:

- reflect on the progress of their work as they design and make, identifying ways they could improve their products
- carry out appropriate tests before making any improvements
- recognise that the quality of a product depends on how well it is made and how well it meets its intended purpose.

Communicate: Let's tell someone!

Assemble a whole-school display of completed items in the hall.
Give classes a time slot to view and discuss the display.

Plenary

Learn from experience: What have I learned?

Consider: Did I learn any new skills during the designing and making? How focused was I during the day? How well did I work with others? How could I have worked better? Was there anything I couldn't do? What do I need in order to be able to do a better job next time?

Notes/implications for future planning

ICT
1 Prepare info
2 Develop/refine ideas
3 Exchange/share information
4 Review, modify and evaluate work

Vocabulary
Gather
Organise
Identify
Generate
Decide
Implement
Evaluate
Communicate
Reflect

Differentiation
By outcome

Support
Give where and when needed

Resources
Planning sheets
Collection of promotional material

Key Assessment

Developing Problem-solving and Thinking Skills in Literacy

NINA SPILSBURY

3

Are you finding any of these perennial problems in your classroom? The proverbial old chestnuts?

> **REFLECT**

You teach it, but it doesn't transfer!

No punctuation, although you've 'done it' many times!

Copies of people and plots from soap operas!

Too many things for children to think about at the same time!

Written work is sloppy and unfinished!

Children make slow progress despite your hard work!

Stale, dull, 'and then' writing!

Poor story endings, although you've 'rehearsed'!

Poor spelling, although you've practised!

Poor presentation!

You set targets but the children ignore them!

'They know what they mean' but can't communicate clearly in writing!

You work towards objectives but children can't tell you what they've achieved!

Children can't identify their problems!

Research is lifted straight off the CD rom!

Children write 'THE END' and wriggle out of redrafting!

Note: The Sudbury Hall TASC project was carried out at Corby Glen Primary School, Lincs.

PURPOSE The purpose of this chapter is to present practical ideas for the alleviation of the learning problems outlined above. While recognising that literacy includes the interrelated skills of talking, listening, reading and writing, the chapter will focus on the skills of writing embedded in a history project, although, obviously, the other literacy skills will be interwoven.

Using TASC problem-solving and thinking skills helps children to learn more efficiently. As the learners gain competence in the recognition of their problems, they are also acquiring the language, problem-solving and thinking skills that they need to deal with them.

Do you agree that children need language and thinking skills to:

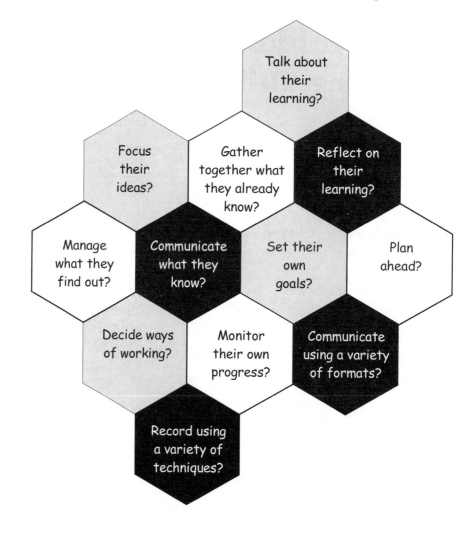

- Talk about their learning?
- Focus their ideas?
- Gather together what they already know?
- Reflect on their learning?
- Manage what they find out?
- Communicate what they know?
- Set their own goals?
- Plan ahead?
- Decide ways of working?
- Monitor their own progress?
- Communicate using a variety of formats?
- Record using a variety of techniques?

COMMENT The language skills, problem-solving and thinking skills outlined above are embedded throughout the learning objectives of the National Literacy Strategy. Some examples of these objectives are shown opposite.

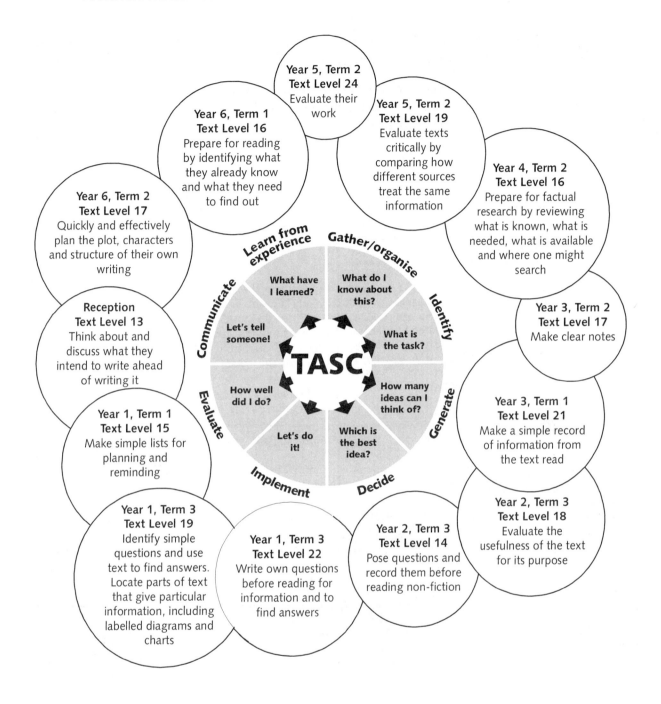

COMMENT

Undoubtedly, all teachers are concerned with developing pupils' language skills, problem-solving and thinking skills. Yet the problems outlined above remain perennial 'old chestnuts'. So how can we extend our practice in order to alleviate the problems outlined earlier? What do we need to do differently in the classroom? How can we more effectively develop the language, problem-solving and thinking skills that permeate the primary curriculum?

It's certainly not a matter of taking on yet another new initiative. Rather, we need to refine and hone what we do already so that our existing good practice becomes more effective.

 We all need to reflect on our current practice in order to recognise what we need to change in order to become more effective teachers.

Take some time to reflect on your classroom practice and give yourself a score for each question, from 10 (usually or very often) to 1 (never or hardly ever).

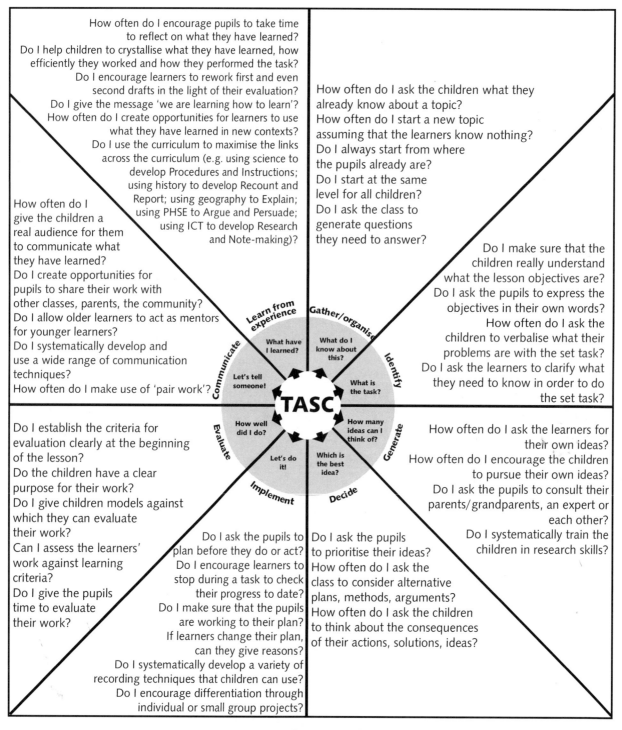

My reflective audit

You may argue that you don't have time for all of the above procedures and questions. However, by helping children to develop efficient thinking processes, by helping them to become independent learners and by giving them a repertoire of learning how to learn skills, you actually save time throughout the year. And, most importantly, the pupils carry the skills with them into successive years. If learners consolidate what they are trying to learn and recognise the skills they are using, they will become increasingly efficient learners throughout their lives. The 'faster' learners will quickly develop and use the skills needed for independent learning; the 'slower' learners will rely on the skills as 'scaffolding' for their developing learning.

When you have completed the reflective audit of your classroom skills, try using a question or a procedure that you don't often use, and gradually widen your repertoire of teaching skills.

Combining Literacy, History and ICT Objectives in a TASC problem-solving project

School Trip to Sudbury Hall, the Museum of Victorian Artefacts

The following project was completed by a mixed group of older Year 4 pupils and young Year 5 pupils. The purpose of the project was to write two accounts of a trip to Sudbury Hall:

- *informally* for a familiar audience – e.g. a close friend – in order to entertain, retell events and inform;

- *formally* for an unknown audience – e.g. an article for the school newsletter – in order to inform, give facts and retell events.

Teaching Speaking and Listening in Key Stages 1 and 2, Learning Objectives (QCA/99/391)

Year 5, Term 2

Speaking for different audiences
- Discuss organisation of material.
- Consider presentation techniques.

Listening and responding
- Identify factual information.
- Analyse use of language.
- Discussion and group interaction.
- Explaining, reporting, evaluating.

National Literacy Strategy Objectives

Text Level Year 5, Term 1

4. Consider how texts can be rooted in the writer's own experience, e.g. historical events and places.
21. Identify the features of recount texts such as historical reports including:
  - introduction to orientate the reader
  - a chronological sequence
  - supporting structures
  - degree of formality adopted
  - use of connectives, e.g. first, next, once.
23. Discuss the purpose of note-taking and how this influences the nature of notes made.
24. Write recounts based on subject topic or personal experiences for a) a close friend, and b) an unknown person, e.g. an account of a field trip.

Sentence Level Year 5, Term 1

3. Discuss, proofread and edit own writing for clarity and correctness, e.g. by creating more complex sentences using a range of connectives, simplifying clumsy constructions.
4. Adapt writing for different readers and purposes by changing vocabulary tone and sentence structures to suit.
8. Revise and extend work on verbs.

Sentence Level Year 4, Term 1

1. Reread own writing to check for grammatical sense and accuracy; identify errors and suggest alternatives.
2. Understand the term 'tense' – i.e. that it refers to time in relation to verbs – and use it appropriately.

Curriculum 2000 QCA History Objectives

Unit 11

What was it like for children living in Victorian Britain? (QCA/98/252)

- Collect information from a range of sources and draw conclusions about the Victorian period.
- Understand that ways of life differed greatly across Victorian society.
- Write an account using historical detail.
- Compare modern and Victorian schooling.

Curriculum 2000 QCA ICT Objectives (QCA /98/211)

- Use ICT to present final draft with suitable layout and presentation.

Introducing the project

COMMENT

It is always important to motivate children to persevere with any sustained effort, and especially with the production of writing that demands that pupils maintain concentration and interest on one topic over a series of lessons. I told the class that we were going on an exciting school trip to Sudbury Hall to find out more about the Victorians. I suggested that as a result of the trip, we could write an informal account to a close friend who missed the trip, or a more formal account for the school newsletter.

As often as possible, I encourage the children to choose to work on a variety of end products so that I can develop a wide range of recording and communicating skills. This also enables me to cater for a wide range of learning styles. But since the aim of this project was to help the children to understand the differences between an informal account and a formal account, there was a need for direct instruction and a specified end product.

Writing, whenever possible, should be for for a real audience provides children with a valid reason for persevering, redrafting and working towards the final product with good effort. So we discussed where we would exhibit our final work and who would receive copies of the school newsletter. After children's work has been exhibited, it is a good idea to bind both the draft and the final versions it into an attractive book and put it in the library for other children to read, and then children soon realise that their work is valued and celebrated. Also, as often as possible, children need to present their work to other classes and to the wider community.

The children also retain copies of their working drafts and final versions so that they can reflect on their thinking and their progress: it is most important to use their working drafts constructively as the means of reflecting on how they have worked and what they have learned. Also, the working drafts are displayed alongside the finished product so that the processes of writing are valued as much as the end product. (And when the children move to another school, they can take their best samples of work to show to their new teacher(s).)

Gathering and organising ideas about what writers need to know

Gather & organise

Adult writers work hard and it is important for children to realise this, so as a class, we discussed how a 'real' writer works and what a 'real' writer needs to know. The children decided that a writer uses 'tools' much the same as an artist or a carpenter uses 'tools'. Then they went on to analyse the kinds of 'tools' a writer needs and their ideas were recorded on a sheet of A1 (see overleaf).

know about punctuation

know lots of exciting words

be able to write sentences

make the story interesting

A writer needs to

work hard

be able to spell correctly

understand the style

have lots of ideas

understand the structure

understand how texts are held together by connectives

hook in the reader

make several drafts to improve the story

Gathering and organising the 'tools' a writer needs

Gather & organise

Gathering and organising everything we know about 'text-marking'

We discussed how we could find out about the 'tools' a writer uses. It was decided that we should analyse some pieces of writing produced by 'real' writers because we were learning to be 'real' writers by producing accounts of our school trip.

The learners used a colour coding system, which we had agreed beforehand, and they worked in groups to analyse the selected passages.

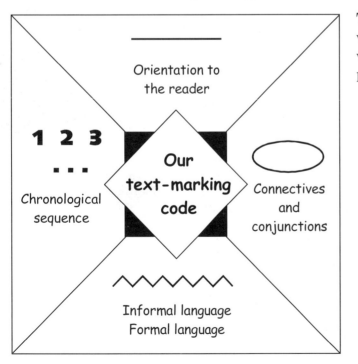

Orientation to the reader

1 2 3 . . .

Chronological sequence

Our text-marking code

Connectives and conjunctions

Informal language
Formal language

Gathering and organising information from an informal account and a formal account

The children worked in small groups to mark the text in the informal account in Passage A, then, as a class, we recorded the characteristics on a sheet of A1 paper. We later followed the same procedure for the formal account in Passage B and wrote the characteristics on another sheet of A1 paper. (We referred to these charts when the class began to write their own accounts after their visit to Sudbury Hall.)

I wrote the two passages, A and B, after my pre-assessment visit to the museum. I wanted to incorporate the main features of the two types of accounts we were dealing with. Whenever possible, it's a good idea to use samples of children's final work from previous years. Using a text that is closely related to the content and the learning objective of the lesson(s) helps children to identify clearly what they are trying to do and then to transfer the skills they are practising. Note that the passages the children were working on had enough space for them to mark the text clearly.

Telling my friend about our visit to Sudbury Hall

As you know, we went to Sudbury Hall last Tuesday. 1(When) we got there, 2 we dumped our bags in an old barn. 3(First) I went to a Victorian schoolroom and I 4 dressed up like a Victorian child. This was great fun! (Before) I went in to the class, I 5 had to pay a penny. (After that) 6 the teacher checked that my hands were clean. (Next) 7 I had to write on a scratchy slate (and) keep my hands behind my back when I wasn't writing. I wasn't even allowed to put my hands on the desk! (Probably) the teacher thought they were too dirty. All that chalk went up my nose! (During) the lesson 8 poor old Micky got told off (and) he had to put a dunce's hat on! Hee! Hee! Serves old bossy boots right! (But) I didn't like the look of the metal ruler (so) I kept my mouth shut. You missed a really good trip (because) we had a cool day out – much better than school.

Passage A:
An informal account of a visit to Sudbury Hall

What have we learned about an informal account?

Usually, after the children's analysis of their text-marking is recorded on sheets of A1 paper, I ask them to extend the lists with any other words they know. With carefully orchestrated questioning, all the children can contribute to an activity like this, and the more able children can extend the others' ideas in a cooperative class effort. When the children have added their ideas, I try to extend their repertoire of words and phrases. As an extension activity, I sometimes ask very able pupils to scan their reading books to find extra words and phrases. However, for the purpose of clarity in this exercise, I used only the words in the passage to analyse the characteristics of an informal account. We talked about the importance of collecting main points in a mindmap in order to help the brain to remember and make sense of what we are trying to learn.

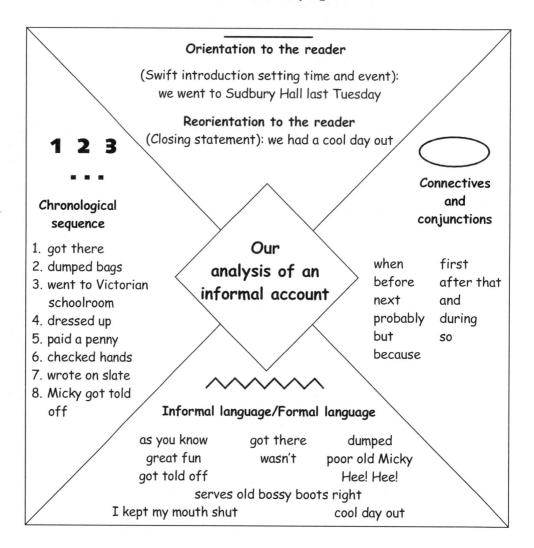

Note: 1. Always use different colours to code the analysis. 2. Most children need help in deciding what are the sequential steps in an account and making a flowchart with key words helps. If the children work on post-it notes first, they can cross out unnecessary words and change the order before compiling their final flowchart.

1a
At the end of the summer term, Class 5 went to Sudbury Hall to experience what it was like to be a Victorian child. **1b** Whilst there, we were given an opportunity to compare the toys of the rich and the poor children, go up a chimney and go through a mine.

Eventually we went to a schoolroom where we dressed up like Victorian children.

2
During the time we were in the toy room, we were able to see Betty Cadbury's toys. She was the daughter of the maker of Cadbury's chocolate, so she had very expensive toys. The most expensive toys were probably the china dolls because they were delicate and beautifully dressed.

3
Next we went to the Museum of Childhood where there was a Victorian chimney and a mine. Here we were informed that poor children had to clean the chimneys and work in the mines. They worked for many hours every day.

Meanwhile, it was interesting to see that poor people lived in very small homes with only one room for two families. The room was dirty and infested with rats.

In the classroom.
The dunces hat   The cane   The steel ruler
Punishments
The toys.
marbles
Rocking horse

4
Finally, we went to the schoolroom where we dressed up like Victorian children. The teacher was very strict and the punishments included the cane, the steel rule and the dunce's cap. We also used chalk to write on slates and we were made to put our hands behind our backs when we were not writing.

We learned a lot about Victorian times and I would encourage you to visit Sudbury Hall.

Passage B: A formal account of a visit to Sudbury Hall

Learn from experience

What have we learned about a formal account?

Using the same procedure as before we compiled an analysis of the features of a formal account and recorded this on a sheet of A1 paper. Note that the formal account is written in paragraphs. Note: use different colours to code the analysis.

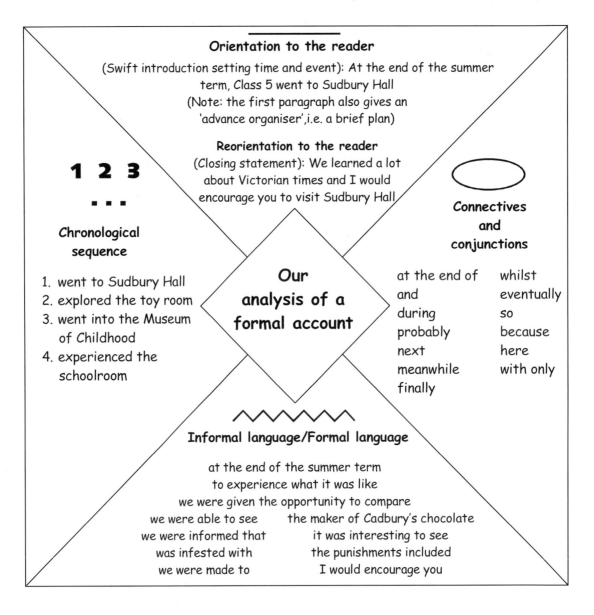

Orientation to the reader

(Swift introduction setting time and event): At the end of the summer term, Class 5 went to Sudbury Hall
(Note: the first paragraph also gives an 'advance organiser', i.e. a brief plan)

Reorientation to the reader

(Closing statement): We learned a lot about Victorian times and I would encourage you to visit Sudbury Hall

1 2 3
. . .

Chronological sequence

1. went to Sudbury Hall
2. explored the toy room
3. went into the Museum of Childhood
4. experienced the schoolroom

Our analysis of a formal account

Connectives and conjunctions

at the end of	whilst
and	eventually
during	so
probably	because
next	here
meanwhile	with only
finally	

Informal language/Formal language

at the end of the summer term
to experience what it was like
we were given the opportunity to compare
we were able to see   the maker of Cadbury's chocolate
we were informed that   it was interesting to see
was infested with   the punishments included
we were made to   I would encourage you

COMMENT ▶

Before our visit to Sudbury Hall, the children were given a blank mindmap so that they could make notes using key words, draw sketches and record impressions and feelings. These mindmaps then became the reference documents for the recounts. NOTE: Take photographs (preferably with a digital camera for getting quick images) because many children become so absorbed during a visit that they forget to make notes. The photographs can then be used to generate key words, moods and feelings and to trigger a memory map.

After the visit to Sudbury Hall, we began our work to prepare the accounts. First, we did a quick revision of what we had learned from the text-marking exercises. Various pupils 'taught' the rest of the class and the children gave excellent presentations referring to the charts we had compiled together. This short exercise clarified the purpose of the task and we were now ready to begin the writing process. Children chose which account they would write and then worked together in pairs. I guided the choice for those children for whom a formal account would be too difficult at this stage.

The procedure we followed is outlined below:

- **Generate** ideas for the recounts of our visit to Sudbury Hall. How many ideas can we think of?

The class worked in pairs to gather ideas for their account of the visit to Sudbury Hall. All ideas were accepted and recorded on sheets of A4 paper. The children used their mindmap notes and photographs of the visit.

- **Decide**

Then the children worked on A4 sheets to decide which were the best ideas for their writing. They drew in their storylines by linking the ideas and numbering them, using a checklist of questions which we generated beforehand to prompt their thinking.

When the children had finished their plans, they shared them with larger groups consisting of about eight children. This activity was an important listening and reflecting exercise. Finally the children were asked to revise their storylines if they wanted to.

Making mindmaps of our visit to Sudbury Hall

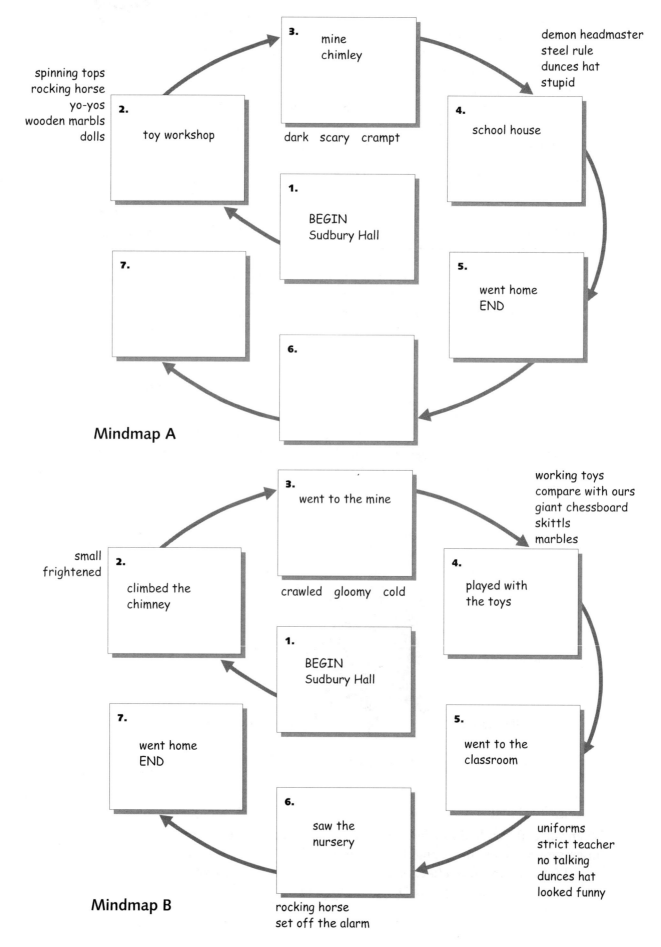

Mindmap A

3. mine
chimley

spinning tops
rocking horse
yo-yos
wooden marbls
dolls

2. toy workshop

dark scary crampt

demon headmaster
steel rule
dunces hat
stupid

4. school house

1. BEGIN
Sudbury Hall

5. went home
END

7.

6.

Mindmap B

3. went to the mine

small
frightened

2. climbed the
chimney

crawled gloomy cold

working toys
compare with ours
giant chessboard
skittls
marbles

4. played with
the toys

1. BEGIN
Sudbury Hall

5. went to the
classroom

uniforms
strict teacher
no talking
dunces hat
looked funny

7. went home
END

6. saw the
nursery

rocking horse
set off the alarm

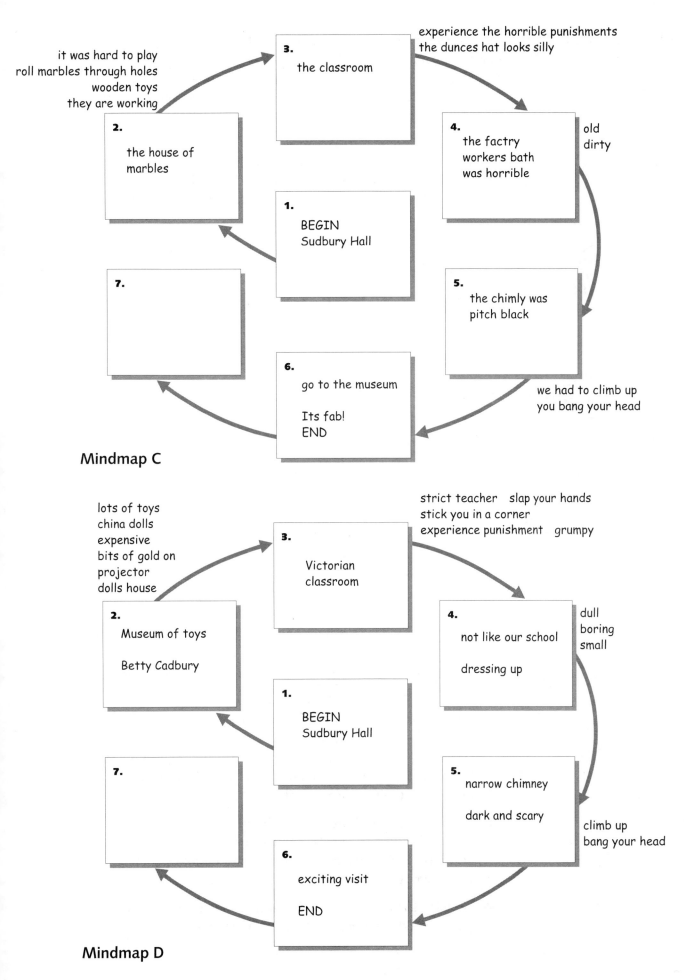

3.
the classroom

experience the horrible punishments
the dunces hat looks silly

it was hard to play
roll marbles through holes
wooden toys
they are working

2.
the house of
marbles

4.
the factry
workers bath
was horrible

old
dirty

1.
BEGIN
Sudbury Hall

5.
the chimly was
pitch black

7.

6.
go to the museum

Its fab!
END

we had to climb up
you bang your head

Mindmap C

lots of toys
china dolls
expensive
bits of gold on
projector
dolls house

3.
Victorian
classroom

strict teacher   slap your hands
stick you in a corner
experience punishment   grumpy

2.
Museum of toys

Betty Cadbury

4.
not like our school

dressing up

dull
boring
small

1.
BEGIN
Sudbury Hall

5.
narrow chimney

dark and scary

7.

6.
exciting visit

END

climb up
bang your head

Mindmap D

COMMENT

Working in this way teaches the children to use key words and phrases, an important skill for thinking and summarising main ideas. It also teaches them how to begin a writing task by considering a range of ideas, and then showing them how to select or prioritise those ideas.

It is important, however, to always make the children aware of the skills they are developing, and to stress 'Think first, plan next and then do the first draft'. (It is a good idea to let the children design their own 'TASC thinking slogans' and to decorate the classroom with these.)

Implement

● **Implement**

Now we were ready to start the writing process. The children need to be encouraged to write their first draft freely, based on their recount plan.

Evaluate

● **Evaluate**

This should be a paired activity. It is important to tell the children that the first step is to remind each other about the features of the account. Also, it is a good idea to remind them that they are working like 'real' writers, such as journalists, editors, novelists and poets.

COMMENT

- The charts showing the characteristics of informal and formal accounts need to be clearly displayed and the children need to be guided to work sequentially through each stage.

- One way to structure pair work is to (privately) rank the children according to their reading ages (1 to 15 in the top half and the lower half), then pair the ones, twos, etc. from each group. Obviously, this is a technique that should only be used occasionally; able children need to work together when it is appropriate, as do the less able.

- The redrafting process needs training and encouragement. The incentive of using 'gel pens' helps, as does working towards a final display or product! Also, you will know how much complexity your class can handle and will obviously adjust the demand of the task accordingly.

- Don't expect the children to make all the corrections, but the second draft will, undoubtedly, be better than the first! Obviously, when you mark, it needs to be in accordance with the learning objectives.

- Go for punctuation first, with each child reading aloud to the partner and *listening* for the natural pauses.

- Next attend to the spelling. A tip here is to ask the children to read their work backwards, then they can give attention to the individual words out of context. Often this makes it easier for them to spot errors. They should first mark the errors with a 'wiggly' line then refer to their dictionaries.

- Usually, when children have mindmapped their ideas, there is not a problem with the sequence of their writing. However, it is a good idea to check against the mindmap, although some children may not have the time (nor be at the appropriate level of competence) to complete the storyline. The mindmap also helps children with paragraphing.

- The last task is to give attention to the connectives and it is important to remind the children not to use the more formal connectives just because they sound important!

- The final draft of the account is produced with a word processor. Of course, the children can work directly with the word processor to produce their first and subsequent drafts, but it is also important for them to 'see' the processes of their thinking and revising so that they can discuss how they worked and how they arrived at their final copy. This is the key stage of reflecting on 'What have I learned?'

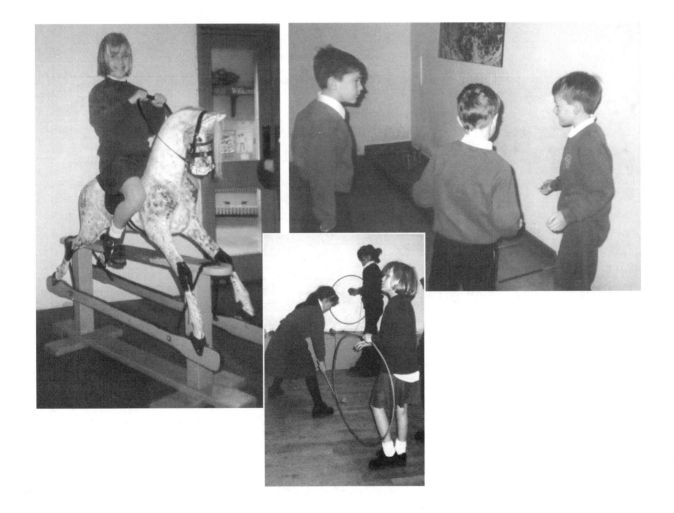

An example of a pupil's redrafting (Mindmap A)

An informal account

1.	
2.	Begin We
3.	Sudbury Hall was a great day out and we had fun! we learnt a lot about
1.	First we
2.	Victorian We We
3.	victorian children. we started on the toy work shop. we played with a big rocking horse,
1.	~
2.	We also played with yo-yos but
3.	and ~~then~~ some spinning tops. ~~and then yoyos~~ not the ones with cogs just plain old
1.	
2.	marbles
3.	wooden ones. I liked the house of marbls best. The idea is to have two tunnels with
1.	
2.	at at EXCITING
3.	big holes on one end and small holes on the other. IT WAS DEAD EXSITING!
1.	Later on Next
2.	~~Then~~ ~~Then~~
3.	then we saw some dolls made of wax and china. then we moved on to the mine and
1.	
2.	chimney. It cramped because
3.	the chimly ~~and it~~ was very crampt and dark and a bit like a maze you cant
1.	
2.	wasn't a Victorian
3.	find your way out. I'm glad I wasn a victorian child. The mine was a bit
1.	
2.	but The
3.	better, I kept bumping my head on the roof. ~~and the~~ worst place was the schoolhouse
1.	
2.	because HAVE
3.	we experienced the demon headmaster STEEL RULES!... ON! THAT MUST ~~OF~~ HURT!
1.	
2.	
3.	The dunce's hat I looked VERY SILLY! Thank goodness it is illegal now!

The procedure that was used for the informal account was used to produce a formal account. Here is an example showing the stages of development (Mindmap D).

COMMENT

An formal account

1.	
2. At the end of the summer term we	Childhood
3. We set off in the morning for Sudbury Hall which is a Museum of childhood. We	
1.	
2.	children.
3. were going to learn about Victorians	
1.	
2. During the morning we	expensive
3. We saw Betty Cadbury's ~~fich~~ toys. ~~and~~ there was a doll's house you could	
1.	
2. inspect	and	that could
3. ~~look~~ in with a torch ~~there was~~ an old type of projector and you/wind ~~it~~ up and watch	
1.	
2.	Meanwhile we were able to compare	such as
3. the monkeys play. ~~We saw~~ the poor children's toys/whip and top, ~~and~~ skittles and jacks.	
1.	
2.	a very strict	was that you could not be
3. We had a lesson with ~~an old grumpy~~ teacher and the problem ~~is you can't be~~	
1.	
2. you would be punished	make you stand
3. naughty or ~~else~~! The teacher would slap your hands and ~~stick you~~ in a corner and	
1.	
2. he would	
3. /call you 'Blockhead'.	
1.	
2.	was different from ours because	also
3. The school ~~wasn't like ours.~~ You had to dress up and it was boring. You/had to	
1.	
2. quietly	
3. sit / with your hands behind your back.	
1.	
2.	
3. We crawled through the chimney and it was very dark ~~and~~ so you banged	
1.	
2. It was interesting to learn that the	
3. your head./ ~~The~~ poor children had to sweep the chimneys to earn money for	
1.	
2.	because I could imagine what it was like to live
3. their families. It was an exciting visit/.	in Victorian times

Here is the final account for the newsletter.

OUR VISIT TO SUDBURY HALL

At the end of the summer term, we set off early in the morning for Sudbury Hall which is a Museum of Childhood. We were going to learn about Victorian children.

During the morning we saw Betty Cadbury's expensive toys. There was a huge doll's house  you could inspect with a torch and an old type of projector that you could wind up and watch the monkeys play. Meanwhile we were able to compare the poor children's toys such as whip and top, skittles and jacks.

We had a lesson with a very strict teacher and the problem was that you could not be

naughty or you would be punished. The teacher would slap your hands and make you stand in a corner and he would call you 'Blockhead'!

The school was different from ours because you had to dress up and it was boring. You also had to sit quietly with your hands behind your back.

We crawled through the chimney and it was very dark and so you banged your head. It was interesting to learn that the poor children had to sweep the chimneys to earn money for their families.

It was an exciting visit because I could imagine what it was like to live in Victorian times.

Reflection on my final draft

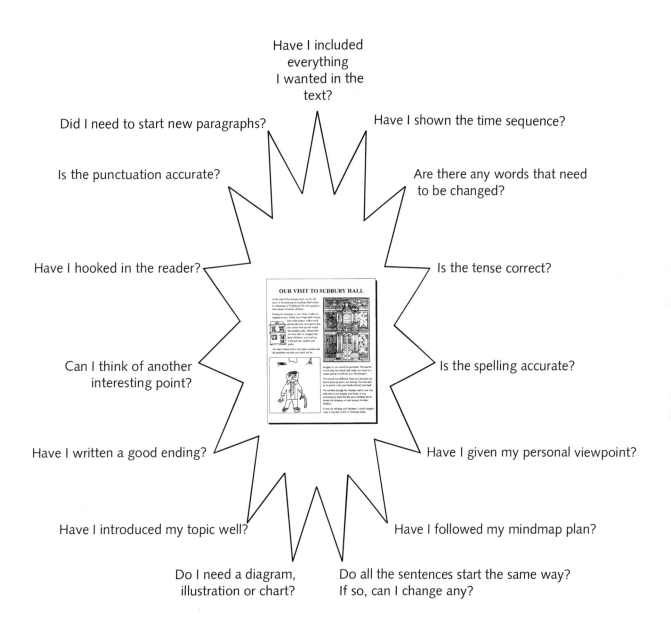

Have I included everything I wanted in the text?

Did I need to start new paragraphs?

Have I shown the time sequence?

Is the punctuation accurate?

Are there any words that need to be changed?

Have I hooked in the reader?

Is the tense correct?

Can I think of another interesting point?

Is the spelling accurate?

Have I written a good ending?

Have I given my personal viewpoint?

Have I introduced my topic well?

Have I followed my mindmap plan?

Do I need a diagram, illustration or chart?

Do all the sentences start the same way? If so, can I change any?

REFLECT!

What have I learned?

What do I need to work on next time?

Checking out the final draft

Begin by asking your partner to read their work aloud. Listen for the pauses that tell you where the capital letters and full stops should be.

Work together to do a spell check. Try reading the work backwards. It often helps!

Golden Rule!
When you read your friend's work, say what you like about it first. A good way to begin is, 'I really like this . . .'

Golden Rule!
Praise your partner if they spot a mistake.

ARE YOU A GOOD RESPONSE FRIEND?

Does the account set the place and time swiftly? Does it have a good ending?

Does the account follow the mindmap plan?

Does the account use a range of connectives?

REFLECT WITH YOUR PARTNER!

What can we do to improve the account?

Developing Problem-solving and Thinking Skills in Numeracy

CHRIS BARRETT

'What do you like best in your Numeracy lesson?'

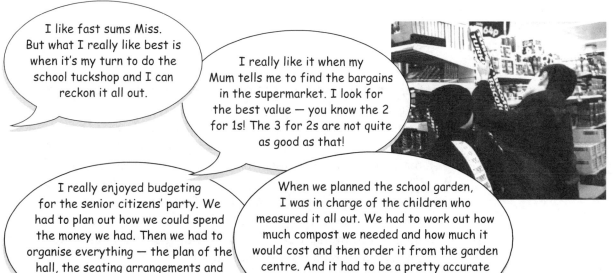

I like fast sums Miss. But what I really like best is when it's my turn to do the school tuckshop and I can reckon it all out.

I really like it when my Mum tells me to find the bargains in the supermarket. I look for the best value — you know the 2 for 1s! The 3 for 2s are not quite as good as that!

I really enjoyed budgeting for the senior citizens' party. We had to plan out how we could spend the money we had. Then we had to organise everything — the plan of the hall, the seating arrangements and how we were going to entertain them. It was great!

When we planned the school garden, I was in charge of the children who measured it all out. We had to work out how much compost we needed and how much it would cost and then order it from the garden centre. And it had to be a pretty accurate estimate because we were working to a tight budget.

The 'Disco' project was carried out at The National School, Lincs.

COMMENT ▶ Although the accent of the Numeracy Framework is on the development of children's basic skills in numbers, calculations, measures, shape and space and handling data, there is ample opportunity to embed the range of basic skills in relevant and exciting problem-solving activities. For me, the essence of the TASC problem-solving model is that it provides a sound and rigorous framework for teaching children how to think actively and creatively while solving mathematical problems related to life. However, this does not mean the children should not engage in 'pure' mathematics for the purpose of the sheer enjoyment and pleasure of exploring patterns and rhythms.

Valsa Koshy (2001) summarises the principles of good mathematics teaching as follows:

- Curriculum materials should encourage the investigation of ideas, questioning and open-ended enquiry.
- Activities should encourage hypotheses, conjectures and generalisations.
- There should be a balance of facts, skills and problem-solving strategies.
- The curriculum should encourage children to go beyond what is being asked in a given task. This will enable them to make connections with previously learnt ideas and also appreciate the usefulness and relevance of mathematics in real life.
- Cut down on the amount of computational practice and make time for in-depth explorations.
- Ensure that children experience all areas and do not concentrate only on number work.
- Make use of the power and versatility of ICT as much as possible.
- Encourage children to take part in competitions and enrichment clubs. (2001: 122)

● PURPOSE The first section of the chapter presents the planning for a series of problem-solving activities related to the usefulness and relevance of mathematics to real life. A practical case study covering a range of mathematics investigations follows, with examples of children's work. The second section of the chapter presents a selection of learning objectives together with examples of problem-solving activities and lists of resources. The activities and possible resources are by no means a finite list but will provide starting points and suggestions for suitable problems and challenges.

Applying the TASC wheel to problem-solving in mathematics

The planning outline shows how elements of the TASC problem-solving wheel can be used for planning investigations in mathematics. The questions are designed as prompts to develop and extend the children's thinking and problem-solving skills.

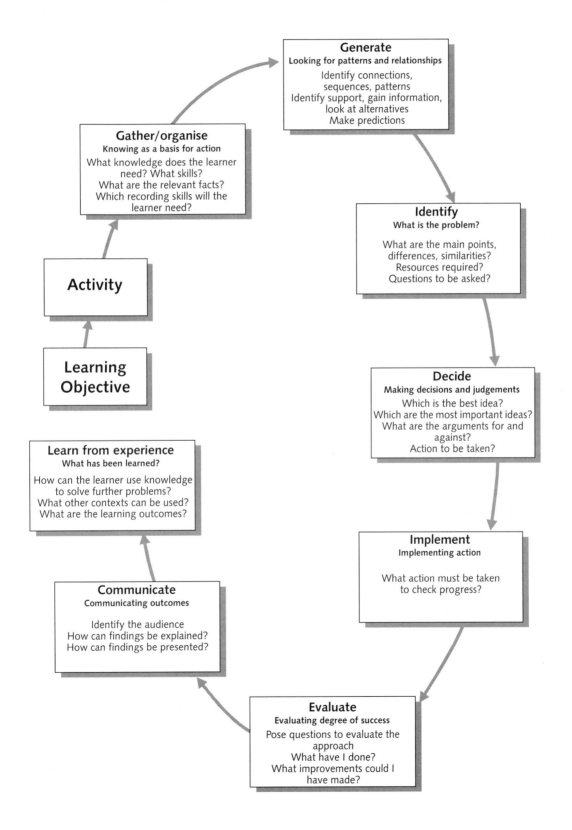

Planning and evaluating the school disco

The children at Key Stage 2 decided to organise their end of term disco and they used the TASC wheel to guide their planning.

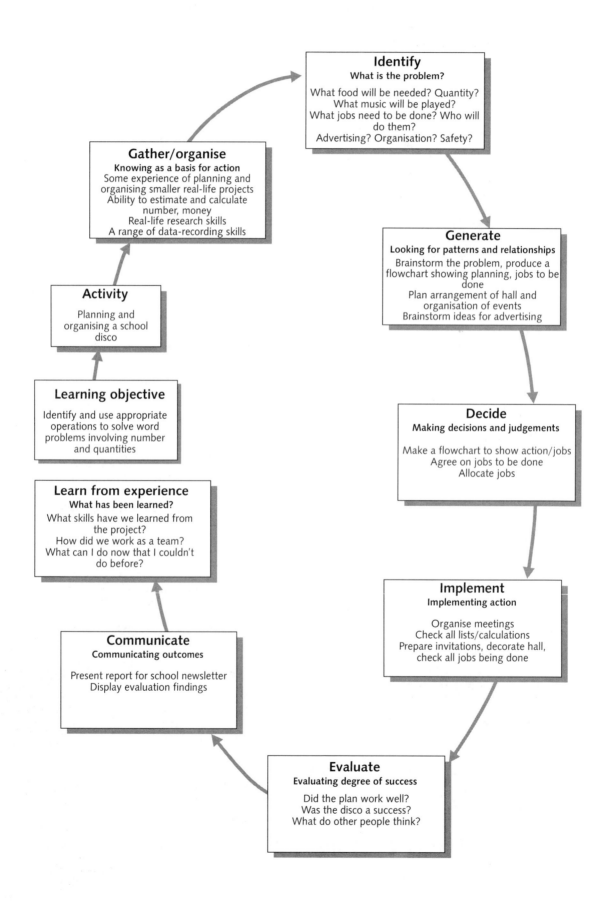

Identify
What is the problem?

What food will be needed? Quantity?
What music will be played?
What jobs need to be done? Who will
do them?
Advertising? Organisation? Safety?

Gather/organise
Knowing as a basis for action
Some experience of planning and
organising smaller real-life projects
Ability to estimate and calculate
number, money
Real-life research skills
A range of data-recording skills

Generate
Looking for patterns and relationships
Brainstorm the problem, produce a
flowchart showing planning, jobs to be
done
Plan arrangement of hall and
organisation of events
Brainstorm ideas for advertising

Activity

Planning and
organising a school
disco

Decide
Making decisions and judgements

Make a flowchart to show action/jobs
Agree on jobs to be done
Allocate jobs

Learning objective

Identify and use appropriate
operations to solve word
problems involving number
and quantities

Learn from experience
What has been learned?
What skills have we learned from
the project?
How did we work as a team?
What can I do now that I couldn't
do before?

Implement
Implementing action

Organise meetings
Check all lists/calculations
Prepare invitations, decorate hall,
check all jobs being done

Communicate
Communicating outcomes

Present report for school newsletter
Display evaluation findings

Evaluate
Evaluating degree of success

Did the plan work well?
Was the disco a success?
What do other people think?

The school disco was a great success! The tasks were divided up between the year groups. There is not enough space here to show all the children's planning and finished work but here are some samples.

Year 3

Investigate how much I can spend at the disco

	25p	10p	50p	£1.00
1.	4 eggs	3 banana	20 juicy lips	50 juicy lips
2.	5 fizzy cola bottles	4 flying saucers	10 chocolate mice	20 fuzzy bears
3.	3 chocolate mice	2 teddies	20 fried eggs	10 fried eggs
4.	2 fuzzy bears	1 teeth		20 chocolate mice

Year 4

Should the DJ play the same music for the Y3/4 disco and the Y5/6 disco?

Y3/4
Rock DJ
Who let the dogs out?
Dream come true
We will rock you

Both
Slim Shady
Lucky
Reach
Stronger
Kids
Deeper shade of blue
Stomp
My love
Oops! I did it again

Y5/6
Hit me, baby
The way I am

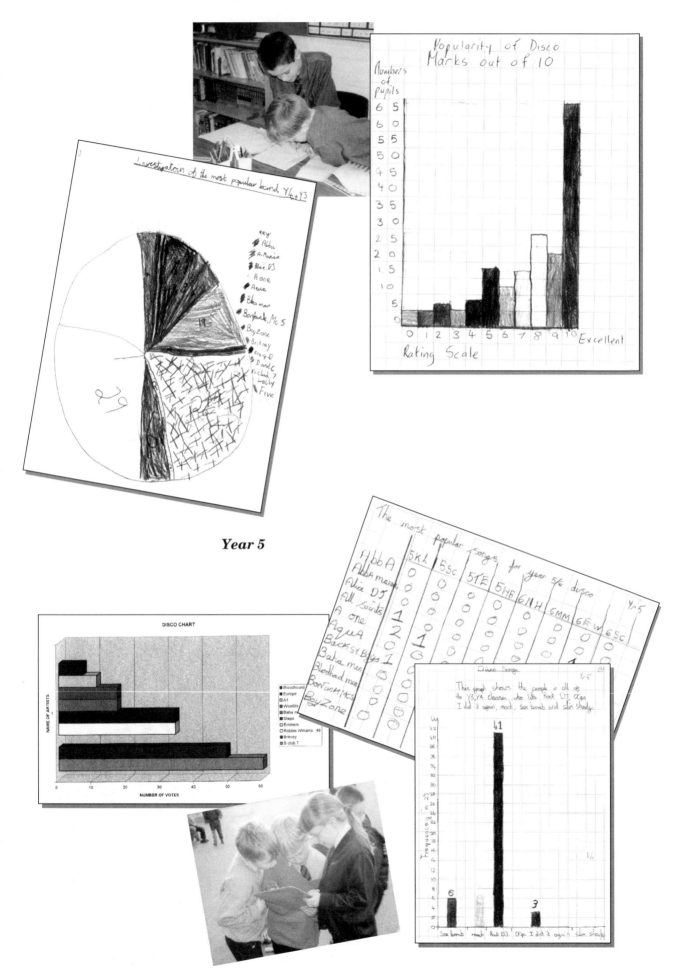

Year 5

Year 6

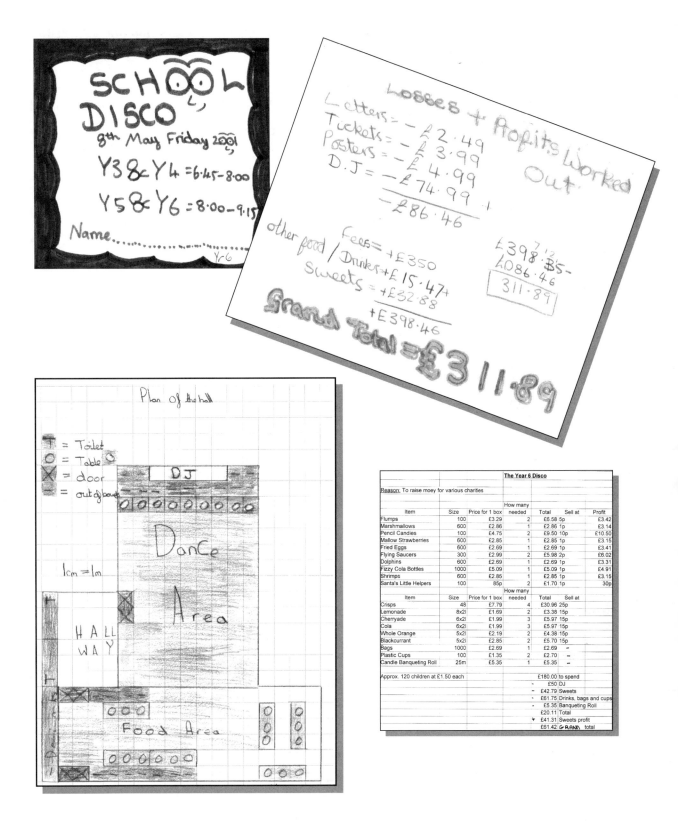

Applying the TASC wheel to problem-solving in mathematics

The questions are designed as prompts to develop and extend the children's thinking and problem-solving skills.

Learning objective	Activity
Solve simple word problems involving measures and explain how the problem was solved. Problems involving time. (Years 1, 2 & 3)	Involve a Key Stage 1 class in planning a visit to the play park. In particular, consideration will be given to timing, sequences and directions.
Gather/organise Knowing as a basis for action	Knowledge of: o'clock, half past and a quarter past the hour, sequencing skills. Relevant facts: start time, length of walking time to the park, playtime, home time. Understanding of: duration of time, days of the week and date. Ability to record using a timeline and label with self-written cards.
Identify What is the problem?	Given only time of arrival at the park and duration time there: What time will you need to set off? How will time be spent on the four play areas? What time will you get back?
Generate Looking for overall patterns and relationships	Concept of fairness: will need directed rotating activities for the groups. If this does not arise, predict/estimate length of time on each apparatus.
Decide Making decisions and judgements	Discuss alternatives for the groupings. For/against fairness of timings. Same result for journey length. Represent on a timeline.
Implement Implement action	Observe sequence of events. Question how conclusions, calculations were reached. Question reasoning behind decisions.
Evaluate How well have we done?	Did we do it the simplest way? How did we work out when to leave school? Were we fair when time was allocated on apparatus?
Communicate Communicating outcomes	Report back to rest of class about the timetabling of the visit. Inform head of visit and time out of school. Transfer timeline to written timetable.
Learn from experience What has been learned?	What similar events could be planned for like this? Information needed for timetable: knowledge, sequence of events. Extend knowledge to bus and timetables and handling data. Evaluate learning objective.

Learning objective	Activity
Solve problems and puzzles in a variety of contexts: shape and space (Years 4, 5 & 6)	Divide a square into smaller squares. Show children the square divided into: (a) four squares; (b) six squares. (The squares do not have to be the same size.) Challenge: Can you devise a way of dividing the square into seven squares? eight squares? Extension: Choose another shape, e.g. equilateral triangle and divide into equilateral triangles. (See Prim-Ed Publishing 1996: 4)
Gather/organise Knowing as a basis for action	Knowledge of the properties of regular shapes. Ability to predict and test. Visual imagery, drawing, cutting and sticking. Ability to measure accurately.
Identify What is the problem?	Keep in mind that it has to be divided into squares. Trial and error by folding, using rulers, scissors and glue. What sizes can the squares be? Is there a relationship between the size of the new squares and the original?
Generate Looking for overall patterns and relationships	Conservation of original shape. What are the possible alternatives? What will happen if I double/halve the size of a square?
Decide Making decisions and judgements	Opportunities to produce sketches, folding, cutting and fitting. Encourage planning as a key to success.
Implement Implement action	Self-check continuously. Share ideas towards a solution.
Evaluate How well have we done?	Have we solved the problem (task)? Did we manage four squares, six squares, eight squares? How far along the challenge did we get? Did our predictions for seven and eight squares work? Did the predictions for extensions work? If not, why not? What were the problems encountered? How were these overcome?
Communicate Communicating outcomes	Present to class or other groups. Publish as puzzle/challenge for others to try.
Learn from experience What has been learned?	Importance of thinking and problem-solving. Practical social skills: cooperation, sharing, etc. Evaluate learning objective.

Learning objective	Activity
Choose and justify the use of an appropriate and efficient method for solving problems. (Years 4, 5 & 6)	Plan, design and investigate the best use of space, money and time to create a wild area and science station with solar powered fountain & wind pump.
Gather/organise Knowing as a basis for action	Knowledge of area/perimeter, times tables, table and data-handling skills. Timetabling. Where to get information. Measuring. Spreadsheets. Calculation of costs.
Identify What is the problem?	Size of plot and size of pond without plot. Which plants to use and how many needed. Providing areas for drawing, science investigations & quiet area. How can we contact people for advice? Budgeting. Resources: Information – fax machine, plants, money!
Generate Looking for overall patterns and relationships	Contact other schools with a wild area. Contact garden centres for advice and help. Match plants with conditions – shade – soil type, etc. Predictions on the number of plants.
Decide Making decisions and judgements	Weigh up different ideas from garden centres and schools – decide on costs, ideas for plants, etc. Weigh up feasibility – database of ideas. Justify why certain plants have been chosen. Timescale for planting. Decide whether to create own concrete slabs or purchase ready made.
Implement Implement action	Draw up detailed plans: • Areas • Number of plants & packets of seeds • Area of paving • Woodchip for paths • Check finances • Measurements for shelter Go ahead!
Evaluate How well have we done?	Look at area and plans. Evaluate area with regard to need, i.e. science investigation, reading area, shelter.
Communicate Communicating outcomes	Write back to helpful schools and garden centres on progress and what has been achieved. Communicate outcomes to governors, head teacher, etc.
Learn from experience What has been learned?	Identify processes and skills that have been learned and how they can be applied to different areas, e.g. budgeting, timescales, communication, data handling/interpretation. Evaluate learning objective.

Learning objective	Activity
Solve real-life problems involving measures and problems involving ratio and proportion (Years 6/7)	Compare/contrast how big their current school/future school is. (A project for Year 6 pupils preparing for transfer to secondary school.)
Gather/organise Knowing as a basis for action	Understanding of ratio/proportion. Understanding of measures: length, area, perimeter, time. Use of data handling: collecting, representing data. Ability to record.
Identify What is the problem?	How big is my school? Identify whether physical size or number of pupils/teachers, etc. Brainstorming exercise. Resources: information on schools (much to be collected by pupils).
Generate Looking for overall patterns and relationships	How wide will your study be? Should we focus on one school or on comparing? Focus on children or buildings? Comparison of time spent and subjects covered at present/future school?
Decide Making decisions and judgements	What will we focus on? Plan of action? Final decision for each child/pair.
Implement Implement action	Periodic presentation of progress. Are studies suitably focused enough? Can we help our peers? Do we need to do a survey? Measuring activity/request information.
Evaluate How well have we done?	How can we demonstrate what we have done? How does this compare to our peers?
Communicate Communicating outcomes	How can our results be presented?
Learn from experience What has been learned?	What do we know about our new school? What lessons have we learned? How could we have presented it differently? Evaluate learning objective.

Learning objectives for Years 1–3 (DfEE 1999a: 62–71)

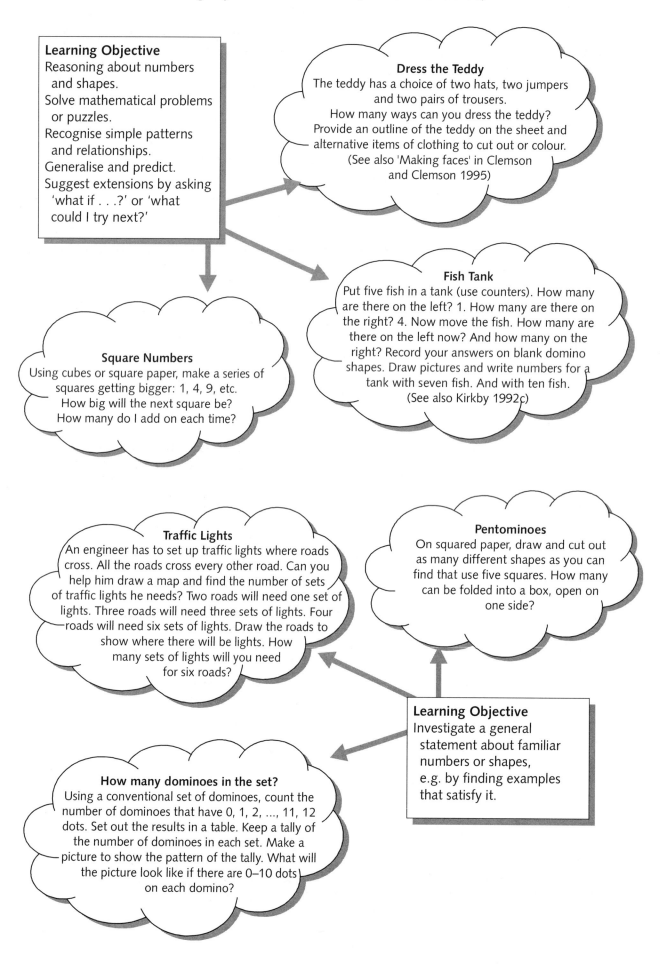

Learning Objective
Reasoning about numbers and shapes.
Solve mathematical problems or puzzles.
Recognise simple patterns and relationships.
Generalise and predict.
Suggest extensions by asking 'what if . . .?' or 'what could I try next?'

Dress the Teddy
The teddy has a choice of two hats, two jumpers and two pairs of trousers.
How many ways can you dress the teddy?
Provide an outline of the teddy on the sheet and alternative items of clothing to cut out or colour.
(See also 'Making faces' in Clemson and Clemson 1995)

Square Numbers
Using cubes or square paper, make a series of squares getting bigger: 1, 4, 9, etc.
How big will the next square be?
How many do I add on each time?

Fish Tank
Put five fish in a tank (use counters). How many are there on the left? 1. How many are there on the right? 4. Now move the fish. How many are there on the left now? And how many on the right? Record your answers on blank domino shapes. Draw pictures and write numbers for a tank with seven fish. And with ten fish.
(See also Kirkby 1992c)

Traffic Lights
An engineer has to set up traffic lights where roads cross. All the roads cross every other road. Can you help him draw a map and find the number of sets of traffic lights he needs? Two roads will need one set of lights. Three roads will need three sets of lights. Four roads will need six sets of lights. Draw the roads to show where there will be lights. How many sets of lights will you need for six roads?

Pentominoes
On squared paper, draw and cut out as many different shapes as you can find that use five squares. How many can be folded into a box, open on one side?

Learning Objective
Investigate a general statement about familiar numbers or shapes, e.g. by finding examples that satisfy it.

How many dominoes in the set?
Using a conventional set of dominoes, count the number of dominoes that have 0, 1, 2, ..., 11, 12 dots. Set out the results in a table. Keep a tally of the number of dominoes in each set. Make a picture to show the pattern of the tally. What will the picture look like if there are 0–10 dots on each domino?

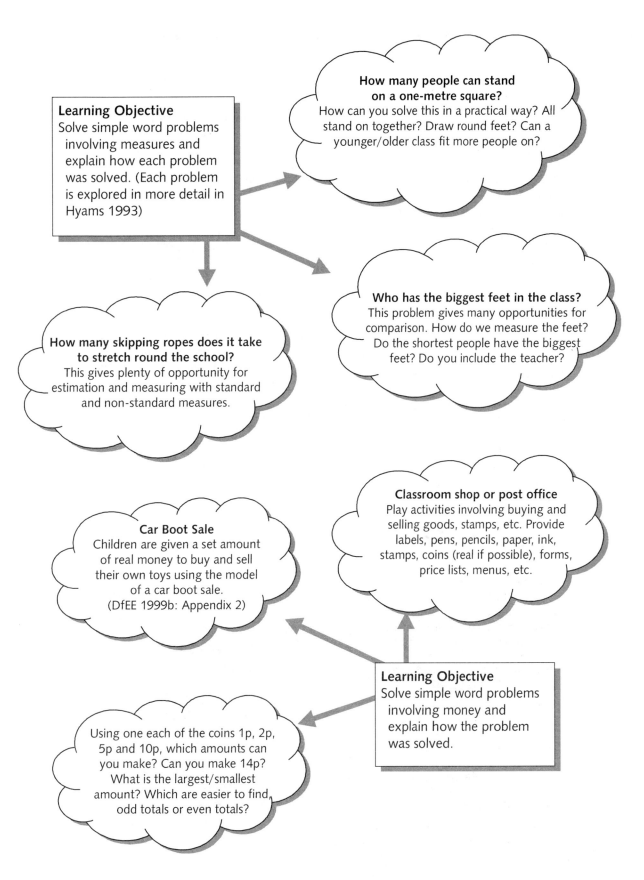

Learning Objective
Solve simple word problems involving measures and explain how each problem was solved. (Each problem is explored in more detail in Hyams 1993)

How many people can stand on a one-metre square?
How can you solve this in a practical way? All stand on together? Draw round feet? Can a younger/older class fit more people on?

Who has the biggest feet in the class?
This problem gives many opportunities for comparison. How do we measure the feet? Do the shortest people have the biggest feet? Do you include the teacher?

How many skipping ropes does it take to stretch round the school?
This gives plenty of opportunity for estimation and measuring with standard and non-standard measures.

Car Boot Sale
Children are given a set amount of real money to buy and sell their own toys using the model of a car boot sale.
(DfEE 1999b: Appendix 2)

Classroom shop or post office
Play activities involving buying and selling goods, stamps, etc. Provide labels, pens, pencils, paper, ink, stamps, coins (real if possible), forms, price lists, menus, etc.

Learning Objective
Solve simple word problems involving money and explain how the problem was solved.

Using one each of the coins 1p, 2p, 5p and 10p, which amounts can you make? Can you make 14p? What is the largest/smallest amount? Which are easier to find, odd totals or even totals?

Resources
Fisher and Vince (1989a), Kirkby (1992c, 1995a), O'Brien (1992), Blinko and Graham (1995), Clemson and Clemson (1998), DfEE 1999a, 1999b.

Learning objectives for Years 4–6 (DfEE 1999a: 78–89)

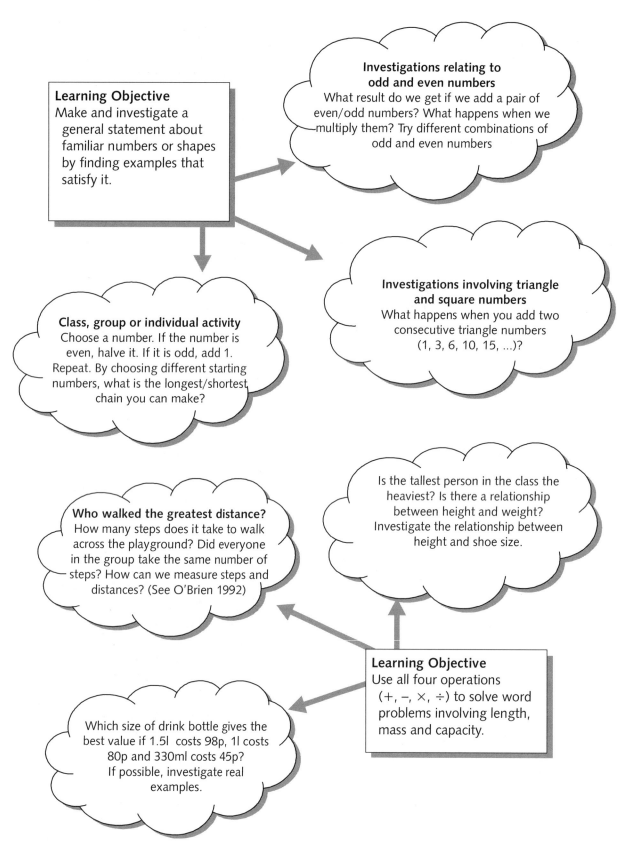

Learning Objective
Make and investigate a general statement about familiar numbers or shapes by finding examples that satisfy it.

Investigations relating to odd and even numbers
What result do we get if we add a pair of even/odd numbers? What happens when we multiply them? Try different combinations of odd and even numbers

Class, group or individual activity
Choose a number. If the number is even, halve it. If it is odd, add 1. Repeat. By choosing different starting numbers, what is the longest/shortest chain you can make?

Investigations involving triangle and square numbers
What happens when you add two consecutive triangle numbers (1, 3, 6, 10, 15, ...)?

Who walked the greatest distance?
How many steps does it take to walk across the playground? Did everyone in the group take the same number of steps? How can we measure steps and distances? (See O'Brien 1992)

Is the tallest person in the class the heaviest? Is there a relationship between height and weight? Investigate the relationship between height and shoe size.

Learning Objective
Use all four operations (+, −, ×, ÷) to solve word problems involving length, mass and capacity.

Which size of drink bottle gives the best value if 1.5l costs 98p, 1l costs 80p and 330ml costs 45p? If possible, investigate real examples.

Resources
O'Brien (1992), Straker (1993), Casey and Koshy (1995), Kirkby (1996), Clemson and Clemson (1998), DfEE 1999a, 1999b, ATM 2000.

Learning objectives for Year 7 (DfEE 2000b: 30–38)

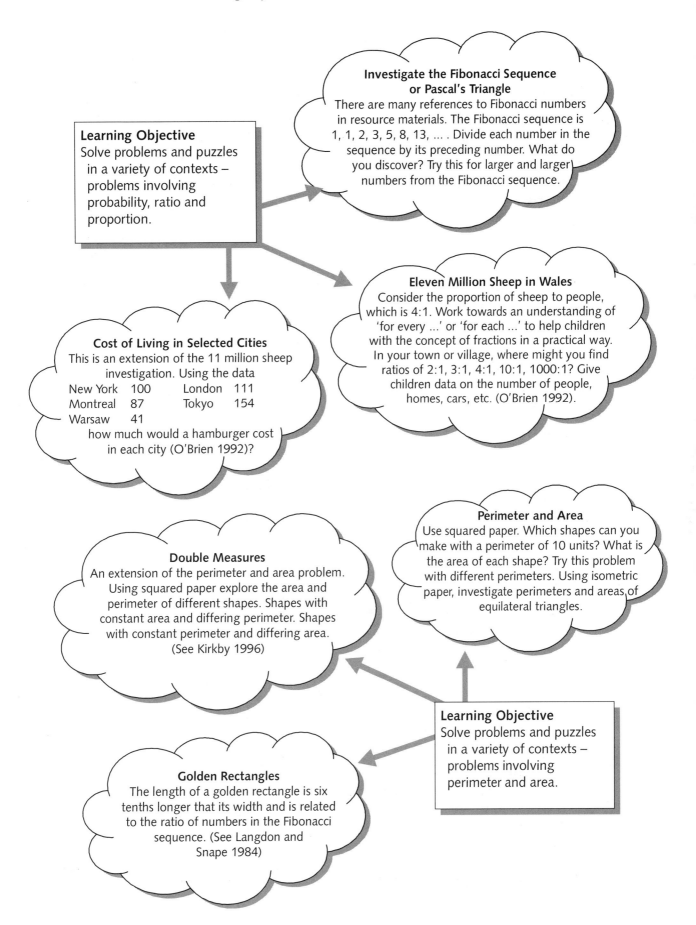

Learning Objective
Solve problems and puzzles in a variety of contexts – problems involving probability, ratio and proportion.

Investigate the Fibonacci Sequence or Pascal's Triangle
There are many references to Fibonacci numbers in resource materials. The Fibonacci sequence is 1, 1, 2, 3, 5, 8, 13, ... Divide each number in the sequence by its preceding number. What do you discover? Try this for larger and larger numbers from the Fibonacci sequence.

Eleven Million Sheep in Wales
Consider the proportion of sheep to people, which is 4:1. Work towards an understanding of 'for every ...' or 'for each ...' to help children with the concept of fractions in a practical way. In your town or village, where might you find ratios of 2:1, 3:1, 4:1, 10:1, 1000:1? Give children data on the number of people, homes, cars, etc. (O'Brien 1992).

Cost of Living in Selected Cities
This is an extension of the 11 million sheep investigation. Using the data
New York   100   London   111
Montreal   87   Tokyo   154
Warsaw   41
how much would a hamburger cost in each city (O'Brien 1992)?

Double Measures
An extension of the perimeter and area problem. Using squared paper explore the area and perimeter of different shapes. Shapes with constant area and differing perimeter. Shapes with constant perimeter and differing area. (See Kirkby 1996)

Perimeter and Area
Use squared paper. Which shapes can you make with a perimeter of 10 units? What is the area of each shape? Try this problem with different perimeters. Using isometric paper, investigate perimeters and areas of equilateral triangles.

Learning Objective
Solve problems and puzzles in a variety of contexts – problems involving perimeter and area.

Golden Rectangles
The length of a golden rectangle is six tenths longer that its width and is related to the ratio of numbers in the Fibonacci sequence. (See Langdon and Snape 1984)

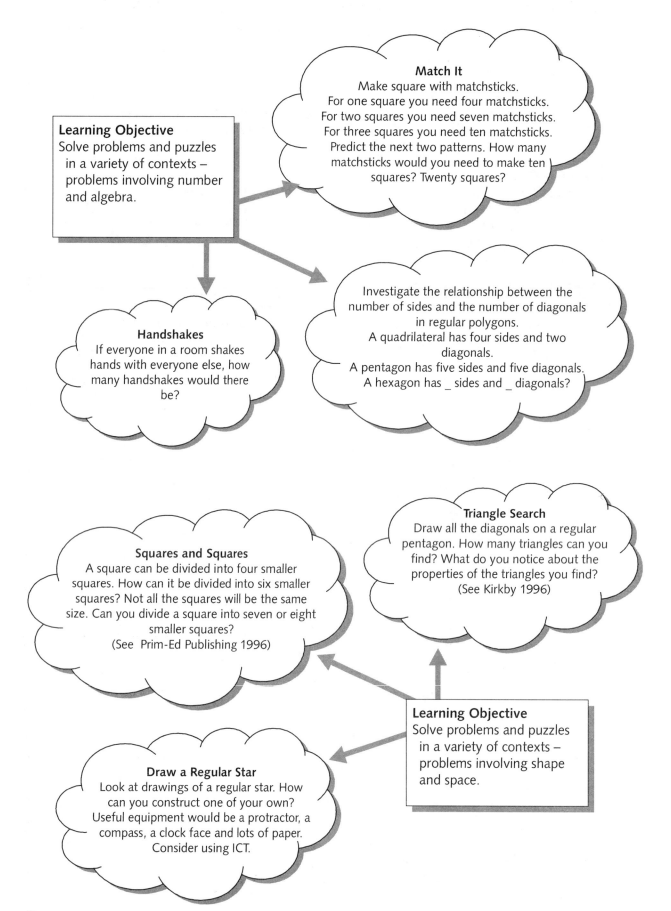

Learning Objective
Solve problems and puzzles in a variety of contexts – problems involving number and algebra.

Match It
Make square with matchsticks.
For one square you need four matchsticks.
For two squares you need seven matchsticks.
For three squares you need ten matchsticks.
Predict the next two patterns. How many matchsticks would you need to make ten squares? Twenty squares?

Handshakes
If everyone in a room shakes hands with everyone else, how many handshakes would there be?

Investigate the relationship between the number of sides and the number of diagonals in regular polygons.
A quadrilateral has four sides and two diagonals.
A pentagon has five sides and five diagonals.
A hexagon has _ sides and _ diagonals?

Squares and Squares
A square can be divided into four smaller squares. How can it be divided into six smaller squares? Not all the squares will be the same size. Can you divide a square into seven or eight smaller squares?
(See Prim-Ed Publishing 1996)

Triangle Search
Draw all the diagonals on a regular pentagon. How many triangles can you find? What do you notice about the properties of the triangles you find?
(See Kirkby 1996)

Learning Objective
Solve problems and puzzles in a variety of contexts – problems involving shape and space.

Draw a Regular Star
Look at drawings of a regular star. How can you construct one of your own? Useful equipment would be a protractor, a compass, a clock face and lots of paper. Consider using ICT.

Resources

O'Brien (1992), Casey and Koshy (1995), Snape and Scott (1995), Kirkby (1995b, 1996), Prim-Ed Publishing (1996), Clemson and Clemson (1998), ATM (2000), DfEE (2000b).

Planning sheet for the development of problem-solving and thinking skills

Learning objective	Activity
Gather/organise Knowing as a basis for action	
Identify What is the problem?	
Generate Looking for overall patterns and relationships	
Decide Making decisions and judgements	
Implement Implement action	
Evaluate How well have we done?	
Communicate Communicating outcomes	
Learn from experience What has been learned?	

Developing Problem-solving and Thinking Skills in Science

NICOLA BEVERLEY

Science stimulates and excites children's curiosity about phenomena and events in the world around them. It also satisfies this curiosity with knowledge. Because science links direct practical experience with ideas, it can engage learners at many levels. Scientific method is about developing and evaluating explanations through experimental evidence and modelling. Through science, children understand how major scientific ideas contribute to technological change. Children recognise the cultural significance of science and trace its worldwide development. They learn to question and discuss science-based issues that may affect their own lives, the direction of society and the future of the world.

(DfEE 2000a: 15)

The recent revision of science in the National Curriculum has resulted in a clarification and sharpening of focus on the knowledge, skills and 'big ideas' included in earlier documentation. The Sc1: Scientific Enquiry programme of study has broadened to encompass a wider range of scientific methodology. Significantly, it requires that children apply literacy, numeracy and thinking skills learned elsewhere in the context of science investigations, enquiries and activities.

Note: The following schools provided photographs and examples of children's work: The Usher Junior School, Ruskington Chestnut St Primary, Grantham, The National Junior School, North Kelsey Primary and Boston West Primary, Lincs.

PURPOSE The purpose of this section is to explore how children's learning in science can be enhanced and extended through the use of the TASC problem-solving framework. Each segment of the TASC wheel has been considered in turn, and practical ideas and guidance for teachers have been included. The chapter concludes with a number of example enquiries that have been addressed using the TASC thinking and problem-solving approach.

REFLECT Many of the strategies mentioned may well be familiar. However, taking time to reflect on what we currently do and to establish ways in which we might extend what we do to maximise children's thinking and problem-solving skills will bring tremendous benefits, leading to raised attainment for all children.

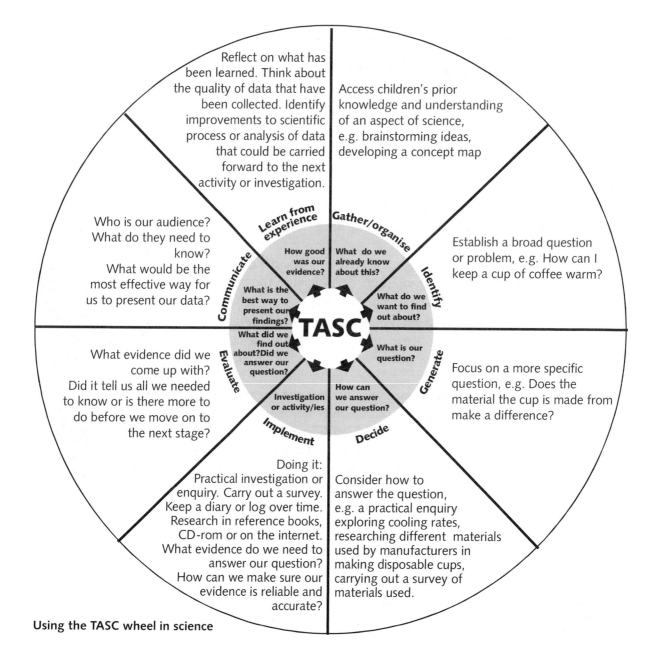

Using the TASC wheel in science

Gather and organise
What do we already know about this?

> **National Curriculum link**
>
> Children begin to make links between ideas and to explain things using simple models and theories.

Finding out what children already know is essential. Use one of the following strategies to establish their ideas.

◀ COMMENT

Concept maps

- Make a concept map of science key words and ideas and link together to form a 'map' of what is known already, or what has been learned.
- When beginning a new unit of work in science ask the children, in groups or pairs, to draw a concept map of *what they already know* about that particular topic. Give them already prepared key words or phrases, or ask them to generate their own.
- At the end of the topic children can review *what they have learned* by drawing a second concept map (frequently used as a review activity in the QCA scheme of work) or by adding to their original concept map using pen or pencil in a different colour.
- Concept maps provide useful information about children's *misconceptions* and *understanding* at the beginning of a topic.

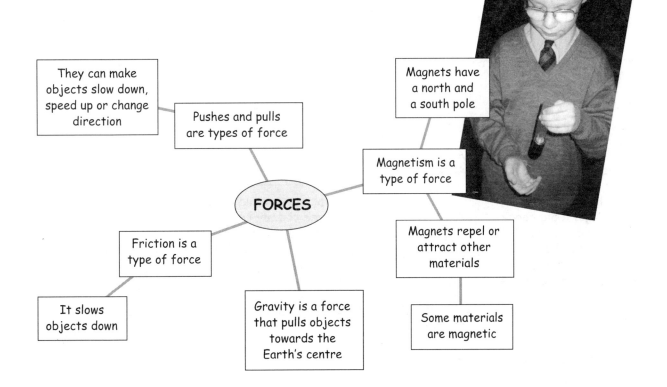

Brainstorming

● Brainstorming scientific terminology, key vocabulary and ideas at the beginning of a unit of work allows children to access their prior learning, whether that learning took place in school or as the result of everyday experience, a hobby or an interest outside school.

KWL grids and QUADS grids

● These grids help children to access and organise their prior learning and think about what they want to find out next.
● KWL grids ask children to write down what they *know*, what they *want to know* and what they have *learnt*. The learnt column is a summary column to be completed after the children have undertaken research on their questions.
● QUADS grids ask children to list *questions, answers, details* and the *source of information*. The answers and details columns can be introduced to children as the short answer and long answer to their question.

K What do I know?	W What do I want to know?	L What have I learnt?
The Earth is a planet. The Earth travels around the Sun. The Earth has a moon. It changes shape depending on where you look at it. Mars and Saturn are names of other planets.	How many planets are there in our solar system? How far away are they from the Earth? Why does the moon change shape?	There are nine planets in our solar system.

Research about the Diplodocus

Q Questions	A Answers	D Details	S Source
How long is its tail? Has it got a big head? What did they eat? Where did they live? How did they reproduce What happened to them?	Yes They ate leaves They lived in North America	Diplodocus were as long as three railway carriages. The tail got thinner towards its end and had 73 bones in it. They laid eggs with hard shells.	CD-rom Dictionary of Dinosaurs

Identify and generate
What do we want to find out about? What question do we need to answer?

National Curriculum link

Sc1 2a: Pupils should be taught to ask questions that can be investigated scientifically and decide how to find answers.

Learning to ask 'good' questions is an essential ingredient for science learning, as all scientific investigations and enquiries begin with a question in need of an answer. Brainstorming questions related to a topic produces many different types of questions. These can provide a starting point for practical investigation or enquiry.

COMMENT

Children will become increasingly confident in categorising questions and identifying how they might best be answered. For example, 'Do fish breathe?' is not 'testable' in the classroom. Research would be a better method of acquiring an answer to that particular question.

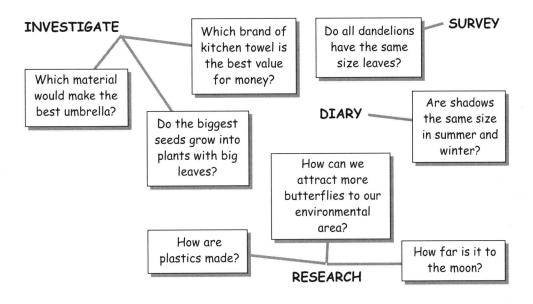

- Different questions require the use of different methods to answer them. Challenge the children to think of ways to answer tricky questions that cannot be answered easily in the classroom.

- Ask children to come up with questions for a homework challenge. These could be related to a particular science topic or random questions as illustrated.

Assessment opportunity

Encourage children to write their own questions on a post-it note as they begin a unit of work. At an appropriate point (perhaps at the end of that topic) they should answer their own question, making use of what they have learned.

- Model the kinds of questions we might ask in science.
- Provide displays around the classroom or a word bank on the work table. Include question stems and example questions that children might ask themselves as they work in science.

Which is best?   Which?   When?

How could we?   How?

How many?   What will happen if?

How big?   Where?

Why?   How does?

What makes a difference?

What question do we need to answer? 'Are bricks waterproof?'

Encouraging children to ask questions related to a topic will increase feelings of ownership and motivation. It is much better to be investigating our own ideas than answering a question given by someone else.

Provide a stimulus question. For example, 'What's the best way to grow plants?' Encourage children to think about their own ideas and use their prior knowledge in suggesting what might make a difference. These discussions will lead in turn to more focused questions to explore. 'Does the temperature make a difference?' 'What growing media produces the best results?'

Make sure that questions chosen are sufficiently challenging by talking with groups of children as they plan. Different groups might investigate a different but linked question. The evidence gathered can be used by all the children in answering their group's question.

Decide
What is the best way to answer our question? How can we get the evidence we need?

> ### *National Curriculum link*
>
> Sc1 2a: Pupils should be taught to ask questions that can be investigated scientifically and decide how to find answers.

The most recent changes to Sc1 have opened up scientific enquiry to encompass much more than practical 'fair testing'. Encourage children to recognise when different questions in science require different methods of enquiry. Often, using a combination of several methods will deepen the evidence base and provide a more comprehensive answer to their original question.

◀ COMMENT

Carry out a **practical investigation**

Research – look for information in **reference books**

Distribute a **questionnaire** and analyse the data collected

Send a **letter** or **email** to an 'expert' to request additional information

Carry out a **survey** and look for patterns in data

What is the best way to answer our question? How can we get the evidence we need?

Collect and consider **relevant information** from leaflets, magazine articles, etc.

Research – look for information on **CD-rom** or on the **internet**

Keep a **diary** or **log** over an extended period of time

Carry out a number of **practical 'tests'** that provide additional information

Ask a local **'expert'** – a friend or parent, school nurse, fire officer, etc.

This list of enquiry methods is a basic checklist. Children can add their own ideas as they become increasingly expert investigators.

Implement
What do we need to think about? How can we collect the evidence we need?

> ***National Curriculum link***
>
> Sc1 1b: Pupils should be taught that it is important to test ideas using evidence from observation and measurement. They should carry out more systematic investigations working on their own or with others.

Planning the investigation

- Which question are we going to investigate?
- How could we find the answer?
- What do I think we will find out?
- Why do I think that? Can I give reasons?
- Do we need to try anything out before we begin?
- What resources and materials will we need?
- How will we use them safely and effectively?

Use these questions with the children as a checklist of things they need to consider each time they work on an activity or investigation. A list added to the back of an exercise book can prove useful.

Obtaining and presenting evidence

- What evidence will we need to collect?
- How will we record our observations and/or measurements?
- How will we record our results?
- What opportunities are there for us to use ICT?

Questions like these are also effective when used to probe, challenge and assess children's thinking.

Working with others to investigate. 'What material could be used to waterproof our roof?'

Considering evidence and evaluating

- What evidence did we collect during our investigation?
- What conclusions can I draw from our evidence?
- Do my conclusions agree with what I thought we would find out?
- Are there any patterns in what we found out?
- How might we improve our work? Was our evidence detailed enough?
- How good was our enquiry?

Evaluate
Do we give children time to think?

National Curriculum link

Sc1 2m: Pupils should be taught to review their work and the work of others and describe its significance and limitations.

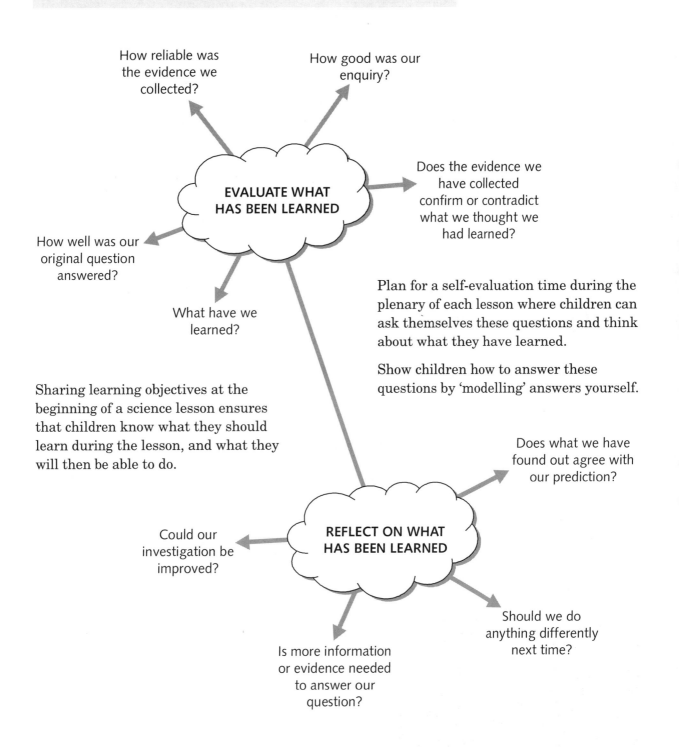

How reliable was the evidence we collected?

How good was our enquiry?

EVALUATE WHAT HAS BEEN LEARNED

Does the evidence we have collected confirm or contradict what we thought we had learned?

How well was our original question answered?

What have we learned?

Plan for a self-evaluation time during the plenary of each lesson where children can ask themselves these questions and think about what they have learned.

Show children how to answer these questions by 'modelling' answers yourself.

Sharing learning objectives at the beginning of a science lesson ensures that children know what they should learn during the lesson, and what they will then be able to do.

REFLECT ON WHAT HAS BEEN LEARNED

Does what we have found out agree with our prediction?

Could our investigation be improved?

Should we do anything differently next time?

Is more information or evidence needed to answer our question?

Communicate
What is the best way to present our findings?

National Curriculum link

Sc1 2h: Pupils should be taught to use a wide range of methods including diagrams, drawings, tables, bar charts, line graphs and ICT to communicate data in an appropriate and systematic way.

COMMENT ▶

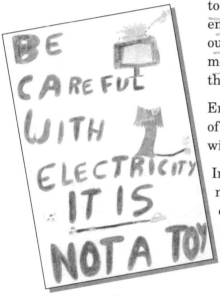

Provide a 'real' reason for children to communicate what they have learned. Examples could be an oral presentation to a visitor, a letter to an expert or a poster for the local community. Having a real audience means that children need to remember the purpose and final outcome of their work throughout their investigation or enquiry. This motivates and challenges children, raising the overall standard of their science work.

Encourage children to communicate their ideas using a wide range of scientific language. Making their own dictionaries and glossaries will reinforce their understanding of this language.

In Key Stage 1, introduce children to different methods of communication and demonstrate how to use them. As children become more experienced, encourage them to choose for themselves the most appropriate way to communicate their findings.

A **newspaper article** arguing why a threatened environmental site should be saved

A **letter** to a sports footwear manufacturer to find out what materials are used to make training shoes

A **diary** logging the growth of a plant or foods eaten over a period of time

A **comic strip** explaining how to make a circuit

What is the best way to present our findings?

A **leaflet** describing how to look after the family pet or how glass bottles are made

A **poem** conveying facts or ideas in an imaginative way

A **poster** warning of the dangers of fire in the home or of playing with fireworks in the run up to Bonfire Night

GERMS

Germs are real ; they make you ill,
They're everywhere and some can kill !
Bathroom, kitchen," They're alive! "
Micro-organisms, microbes thrive.
Bad and good,
On your food,
Beware, beware, beware, beware!
Those nasty germs are everywhere!

Joe; Kieran & James

the light goes to
the person and
It blocks the light
and forms a shadow.

Dear Diary,
We were the Solar system today;
We made it outside, after play.
Peter was Pluto – the furthest planet,
Jupiter was acted out by Janet.

The rest of us stood and waited for a part,
I wanted to be Mars with all of my heart!
BUT . . .

Michael was Mercury, Venus was Vicky,
Emma was Earth, Neptune was Nicky,
Susan was Saturn, and Uranus was Ricky.

Only one left, only one part,
I wanted to be Mars with all of my heart.
I stood there waiting, with everything crossed,
The teacher said, 'Something seems to be lost!'

She looked at me, she looked at Lars,
And said to HIM, 'You can be Mars'.
The 'Planets' went and took their places,
With chattering voices and joyful faces.

Teacher said, 'When we've begun,
You need to orbit round the Sun'.
'But Miss!' we cried, 'We've forgotten TWO!
The Moon and Sun.' 'The Moon can be YOU.'
She said to the smallest boy called Lee.
'And you can be the Sun,' she said to ME!

'Hold out your fingers, make yourself big,
Stand quite still like a branching twig!'

So there I stood, feet firm on the ground,
While all the planets orbited round.
I was the STAR, I was the Sun!
For me the fun had just begun.

I guess we'd still be there as well
But the lesson was cut by the home-time bell.
I left the field with a feeling of sorrow,

I BET WE'LL WRITE ABOUT IT TOMORROW!

Communicating through poetry

Drawings

- Record what has been observed during an activity or investigation.
- Communicate simple ideas and understanding using few words.
- Illustrate more complex ideas to aid explanation.

Diagrams

- Include only essential information.
- Represent objects formally, clearly labelled, e.g. circuit diagrams.
- Use colour selectively. If the colour in a diagram or graph does not help someone to understand it, its use needs rethinking.

Tables

- Record numbers, words or pictures.
- Design and draft tables on paper or using a computer.

Graphs

- Physically graph results using objects, building blocks or multilink cubes.
- Construct simple block graphs or complex line graphs when appropriate to present data.
- Apply knowledge of how to construct graphs in the context of a science investigation.

ICT

- Word-process reports of investigations, produce leaflets, instructions, etc.
- Input information into a database.
- Record data in the environment using data-loggers with electronic sound, light and temperature sensors.
- Convert data into different forms, e.g. a table of information to a bar graph or pie chart.

 Why not write up a science investigation or enquiry during the literacy hour? Focus on how to organise the writing, select appropriate scientific vocabulary and choose the best tone (formal or informal). Many children will be able to use the model independently as they work. Others may need the support of a writing frame for a time.

Developing children's science writing

Children need to learn how to write in a variety of ways if they are to communicate their work effectively.

Writing frames:

- provide children with a skeleton outline of words, questions or phrases;
- offer support without the teacher working directly with the child;
- increase children's confidence and independence;
- support children of different abilities as they learn, but can also be used to extend thinking further;
- eventually lead to children writing independently.

What I want to find out is...

Do plants need soil to grow?

This is what I will do...
Water the seeds, give them sunlight and give them the right temperature,

---

Instructions for growing seed

Type of seed: Price:

You will need:

What to do

First . . .

Next . . .

Then . . .

Your seedlings will need these things to grow:

What I have learnt

I already knew that:
If you put a north and north or south and south part of a magnet together they would repel.

I have learnt that:
Magnets are very useful because if a man got iron in his eye the doctor could use a magnet to get it out. There is a magnetic field but you can't see it. Lodestone was the first magnet.

The most interesting thing I found out is:
I think the most interesting thing I learned about a magnet was that it could work through water.

This is what I found out...

Plants grow faster in soil but can also grow in other things like leaves, sand, cotton wool, and in paper towels.

Learn from experience
Do we give children time to think about what they have learned and apply it to a different context?

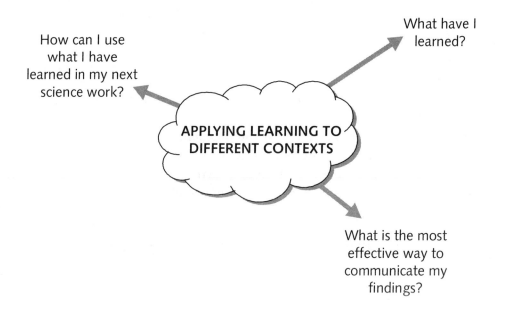

How can I use what I have learned in my next science work?

What have I learned?

APPLYING LEARNING TO DIFFERENT CONTEXTS

What is the most effective way to communicate my findings?

- Plan a 'pathway' of activities and investigations that encourage children to recognise links between knowledge, skills and ideas.
- Provide 'real-life' problems to solve that require children to apply what they have already learned.
- Encourage children to think about what they have learned during an investigation or an enquiry and reflect on how they might improve the next one they do.
- Provide opportunities to use and apply skills learned – e.g. using a thermometer – choosing how to record evidence, in the context of an investigation or enquiry.
- Challenge children to communicate their ideas, knowledge and understanding through poetry, newspaper reports, leaflets, posters, comic strips, etc.
- Help children to make links between the things they have learned using a concept map of key vocabulary and ideas.

'What makes the walls waterproof?'

Starting point

The school was having a new brick extension built. The entire building process had been closely observed by the children, who had generated their own question in this context.
What makes the walls waterproof?

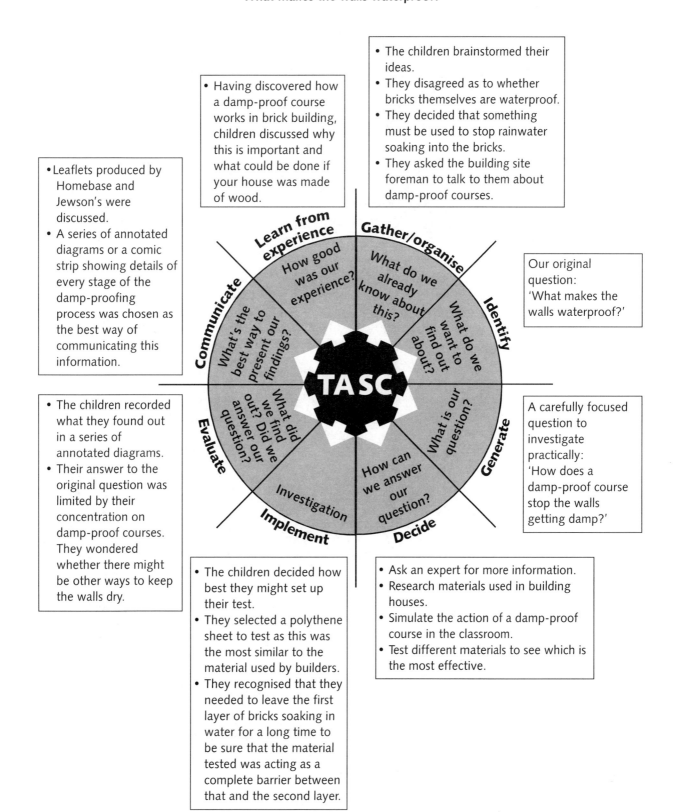

- Having discovered how a damp-proof course works in brick building, children discussed why this is important and what could be done if your house was made of wood.

- The children brainstormed their ideas.
- They disagreed as to whether bricks themselves are waterproof.
- They decided that something must be used to stop rainwater soaking into the bricks.
- They asked the building site foreman to talk to them about damp-proof courses.

- Leaflets produced by Homebase and Jewson's were discussed.
- A series of annotated diagrams or a comic strip showing details of every stage of the damp-proofing process was chosen as the best way of communicating this information.

Our original question:
'What makes the walls waterproof?'

- The children recorded what they found out in a series of annotated diagrams.
- Their answer to the original question was limited by their concentration on damp-proof courses. They wondered whether there might be other ways to keep the walls dry.

A carefully focused question to investigate practically:
'How does a damp-proof course stop the walls getting damp?'

- The children decided how best they might set up their test.
- They selected a polythene sheet to test as this was the most similar to the material used by builders.
- They recognised that they needed to leave the first layer of bricks soaking in water for a long time to be sure that the material tested was acting as a complete barrier between that and the second layer.

- Ask an expert for more information.
- Research materials used in building houses.
- Simulate the action of a damp-proof course in the classroom.
- Test different materials to see which is the most effective.

'Which washing-up liquid is the best?'

Starting point

A local cafe manager explained the need for good hygiene in washing up. She talked to the children about the difficulty of ensuring that plates are really clean, and set the problem:

How can we get our plates really clean?

- Each group thought about the information they needed to tell their audience (the cafe manager).
- They tried to make sure that their evidence was good enough to convince them that their findings could be believed.
- They reflected that additional information would have been helpful to back up their practical research.

- The children decided that they could best communicate their findings through a written report and an advertising poster.
- Children were challenged to consider which aspects of their investigation they should include in their written report.
- They considered putting information into sections and using tables where appropriate.
- Each group considered the purpose and content of their advertising posters.
- They ensured that their use of colour and layout attracted attention.

- The children brainstormed (with teacher support) what might affect the way a washing-up liquid performs.
- They came up with:
  - temperature of the water
  - amount of water
  - type of washing-up liquid
  - amount of washing-up liquid.

Our original question: 'How can the cafe get their plates really clean?'

- Each group recorded their results in a table and a graph.
- They discussed their findings with each other.

A carefully focused question to investigate practically: 'Which washing-up liquid is the most effective at removing grease from plates?'

- The class discussed and agreed how they were going to carry out the practical investigation, including exactly how to wash the dishes.
- They discussed how they could provide evidence for each plate. They designed a standard grid, which was used to measure the area of the plate that was still greasy.

- Test a selection of washing-up liquids, taking account of price and amount needed.
- Write to several manufacturers for further information.
- Carry out a survey/opinion poll of mums' views.

TASC wheel: Learn from experience — How good was our experience? / Gather/organise — What do we already know about this? / Identify — What do we want to find out about? / Generate — What is our question? / Decide — How can we answer our question? / Implement — Investigation / Evaluate — What did we find out? Did we answer our question? / Communicate — What's the best way to present our findings?

'How can we keep frozen food cold?'

Starting point

A local frozen food manufacturer talked to a class of children about the design of packaging. He asked them:
What is the best material for packaging frozen food?

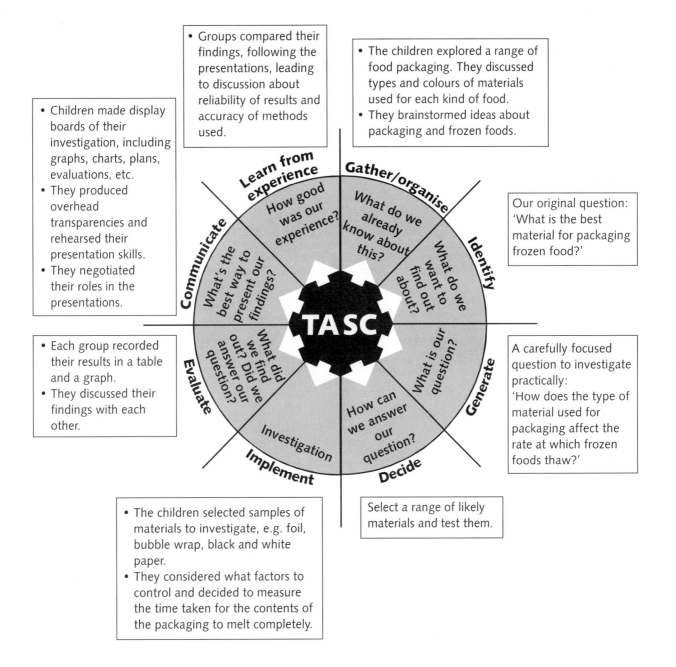

- Groups compared their findings, following the presentations, leading to discussion about reliability of results and accuracy of methods used.

- The children explored a range of food packaging. They discussed types and colours of materials used for each kind of food.
- They brainstormed ideas about packaging and frozen foods.

- Children made display boards of their investigation, including graphs, charts, plans, evaluations, etc.
- They produced overhead transparencies and rehearsed their presentation skills.
- They negotiated their roles in the presentations.

Our original question: 'What is the best material for packaging frozen food?'

- Each group recorded their results in a table and a graph.
- They discussed their findings with each other.

A carefully focused question to investigate practically: 'How does the type of material used for packaging affect the rate at which frozen foods thaw?'

- The children selected samples of materials to investigate, e.g. foil, bubble wrap, black and white paper.
- They considered what factors to control and decided to measure the time taken for the contents of the packaging to melt completely.

Select a range of likely materials and test them.

Developing Problem-solving and Thinking Skills through an Art and Literacy Project

VICTORIA HONEYWOOD

This above all: to thine own self be true,
And it must follow, as the night the day,
Thou canst not then be false to any man.
W. Shakespeare, Hamlet, *Act 1 Scene 3*

Throughout my career I believe that I have always encouraged children to use problem-solving and thinking skills to plan and organise their ideas, to question themselves about their work and to evaluate and edit as they do so. On occasions, this can be frustrating because it takes time for children to become competent in using these skills; but the time spent and the effort invested is worthwhile since the children become both competent and confident in using a repertoire of 'learning how to learn' skills. Alongside the development of pupils' capacity to think for themselves is the equally important development of self-esteem and self-confidence. It is essential to help all learners to understand and value themselves as unique and worthwhile individuals. The development of emotional intelligence must be congruent with the development of intellectual intelligence.

Encouraging children to develop the skills of thinking for themselves is professionally challenging because the children need to be given open-ended questions and as few predetermined answers as is

Note: The TASC project was carried out at Corby Glen Primary School, Lincs.

possible. Mediation and interaction is time consuming and children also need the time to practise finding answers for themselves. Moreover, while many children happily take up the challenge of investigation and research, others feel 'safer' with a straightforward activity with a right or wrong answer and need to develop the confidence to explore alternative methods and solutions.

However, the rewards of working with children who are developing into independent and sophisticated learners is tremendous. When children begin to transfer problem-solving strategies and thinking skills across the curriculum and are excited about what they have achieved, I am reinforced in my role as a teacher, who is an *enabler*.

My approach to teaching has always been largely intuitive – a 'feel' for what children need. However, the TASC problem-solving wheel and the tools for effective thinking have provided me with a sound research base and a more coherent structure, which has enabled me to reflect on, consolidate and extend my classroom practice.

For example, I had not previously considered that if we want to encourage independent learning we must openly discuss with the children the processes and skills that they are utilising at each stage of their work; thus developing their 'thinking skills' awareness together with the appropriate vocabulary. If they are 'gathering and organising' information then that is what we call the process; if they are 'evaluating' while editing, then we must point that out also.

With the introduction of the National Curriculum and the pressure of SATs, we have all found it much more difficult to work in this way. Some pressures have been lifted with the emergence of 'Curriculum 2000'. Links between subjects are encouraged again and we are asked to teach children a repertoire of thinking skills. We can all feel heartened that we are now being encouraged to teach children skills that are essential life skills and to work in a way that good primary schools have always found successful for the motivation and development of the children in our care.

My reasons for teaching problem-solving and thinking skills
Can you add any more?

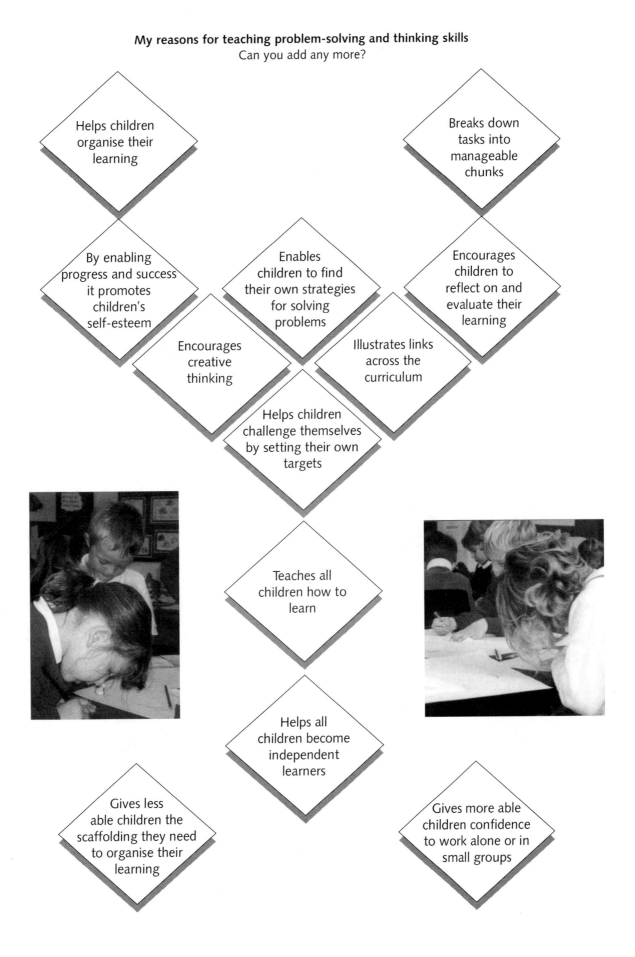

Helps children organise their learning

Breaks down tasks into manageable chunks

By enabling progress and success it promotes children's self-esteem

Enables children to find their own strategies for solving problems

Encourages children to reflect on and evaluate their learning

Encourages creative thinking

Illustrates links across the curriculum

Helps children challenge themselves by setting their own targets

Teaches all children how to learn

Helps all children become independent learners

Gives less able children the scaffolding they need to organise their learning

Gives more able children confidence to work alone or in small groups

The development of problem-solving and thinking skills at our school has progressed in several stages. This mindmap illustrates the progression:

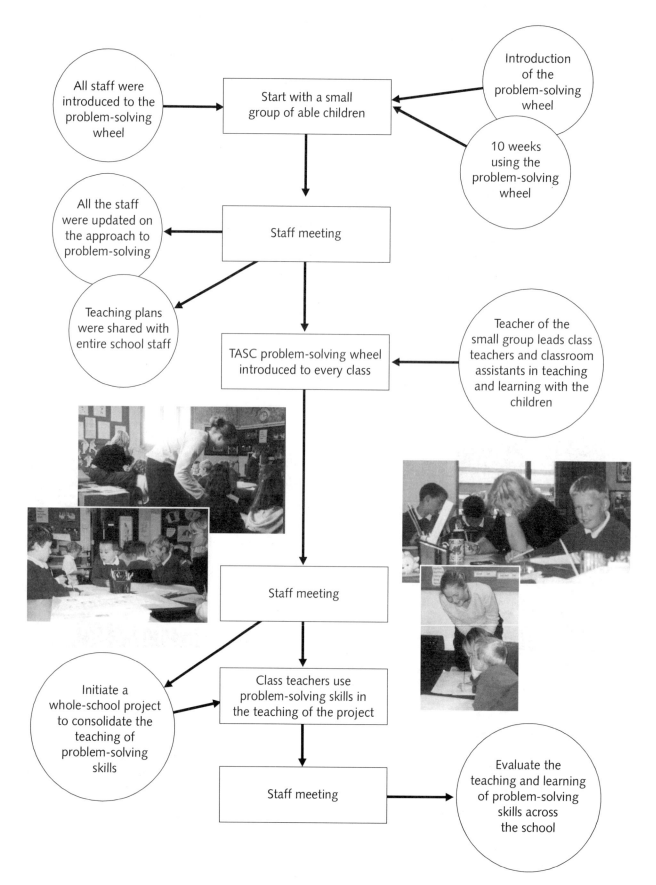

Stage 1: Introducing the TASC wheel to a group of children

The teaching of problem-solving and thinking skills is being developed for all the children in our school but the TASC problem-solving wheel was first trialled with a group of able children in Year 3. The TASC wheel was used as the focus for an extension project covering a variety of activities. The children showed extensive improvement in their levels of concentration, their ability to focus on a task in depth and their willingness to cooperate with one another. The mindmap on page 110 is a record of what was done.

The children were introduced to the TASC problem-solving wheel and the cycle of skills discussed. The aim was to practise those skills. Gathering and organising information, identifying the task, generating ideas and deciding on the best one were identified as important elements of successful planning. Having implemented their ideas and completed the task, the children evaluated what they had done. We discussed whether they had reached the goal they set themselves at the identifying stage. We discussed which skills they had practised and learned from each activity so that those skills could be clearly identified and called on again when tackling a new task. It was decided that they could communicate (display, perform, etc.) if appropriate but that they may not always wish to do so.

There were many positive outcomes resulting from the ten weeks with the initial group of children. The child who had difficulty in applying himself to a given task and concentrating for any length of time became more confident about approaching tasks independently and became less disruptive. His self-esteem grew as he became more successful and he was enthusiastic to work. He, in particular, found mindmapping a useful tool since he used it for 'maximum thinking and minimum recording'.

One child found working in a small group very frustrating because she wanted to be in control and take on many roles within it. However, she learned much about herself and discovered how a group can function successfully. She was able to participate in a role-play story to support her writing. She worked with enthusiasm and consideration with a partner when designing a game to help other children learn a body of knowledge in science.

All the children became familiar with the stages of the TASC wheel and used them appropriately and successfully to solve problems and complete tasks. All used mindmaps and were able to edit their writing and were extremely pleased to see the improvements they made.

It was inspirational to watch children communicating successfully with each other and finding various methods to organise and carry out specific tasks. To see children's confidence and self-esteem flourish as they successfully attain their goals was confirmation that teaching children problem-solving and thinking skills is essential.

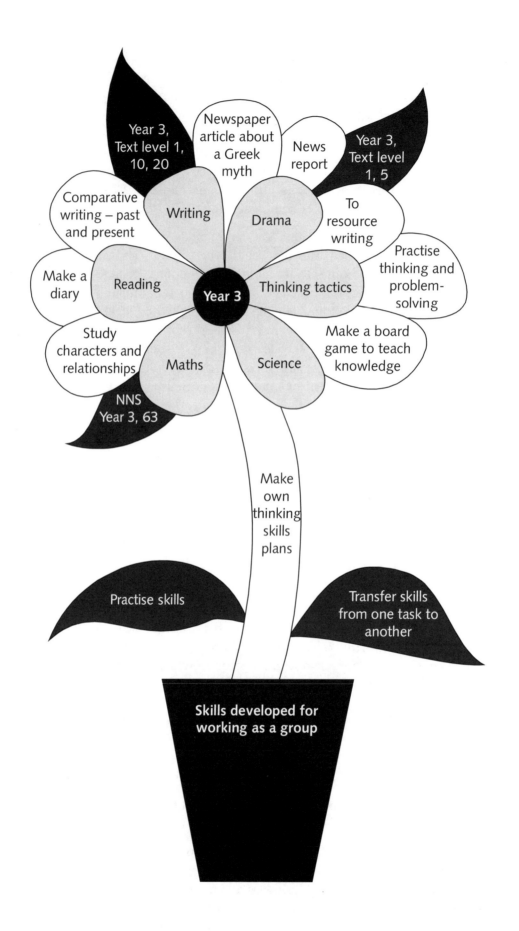

Examples of planning and writing based on Greek mythology

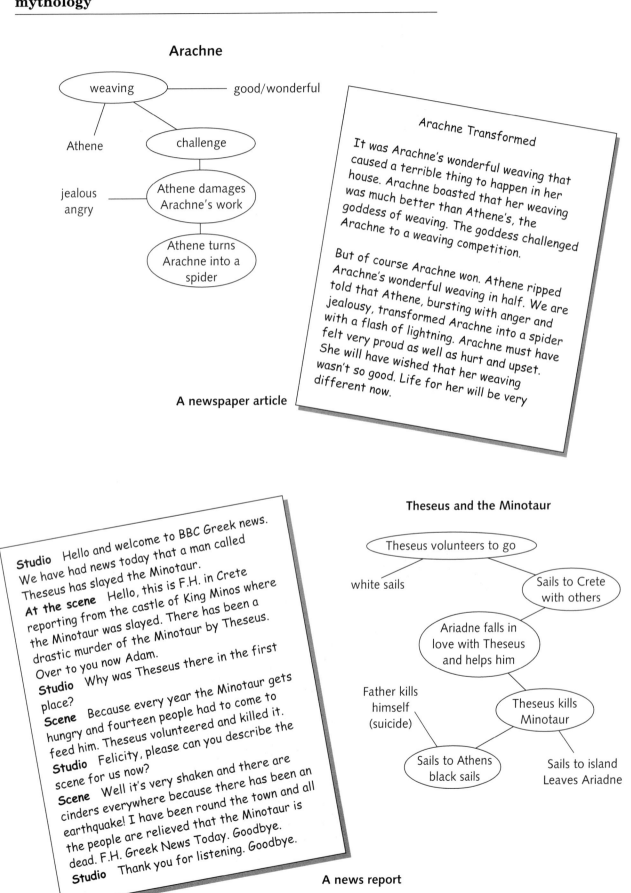

Arachne

weaving — good/wonderful

Athene

challenge

jealous
angry

Athene damages
Arachne's work

Athene turns
Arachne into a
spider

A newspaper article

Arachne Transformed

It was Arachne's wonderful weaving that caused a terrible thing to happen in her house. Arachne boasted that her weaving was much better than Athene's, the goddess of weaving. The goddess challenged Arachne to a weaving competition.

But of course Arachne won. Athene ripped Arachne's wonderful weaving in half. We are told that Athene, bursting with anger and jealousy, transformed Arachne into a spider with a flash of lightning. Arachne must have felt very proud as well as hurt and upset. She will have wished that her weaving wasn't so good. Life for her will be very different now.

Studio Hello and welcome to BBC Greek news. We have had news today that a man called Theseus has slayed the Minotaur.
At the scene Hello, this is F.H. in Crete reporting from the castle of King Minos where the Minotaur was slayed. There has been a drastic murder of the Minotaur by Theseus. Over to you now Adam.
Studio Why was Theseus there in the first place?
Scene Because every year the Minotaur gets hungry and fourteen people had to come to feed him. Theseus volunteered and killed it.
Studio Felicity, please can you describe the scene for us now?
Scene Well it's very shaken and there are cinders everywhere because there has been an earthquake! I have been round the town and all the people are relieved that the Minotaur is dead. F.H. Greek News Today. Goodbye.
Studio Thank you for listening. Goodbye.

A news report

Theseus and the Minotaur

Theseus volunteers to go

white sails

Sails to Crete
with others

Ariadne falls in
love with Theseus
and helps him

Father kills
himself
(suicide)

Theseus kills
Minotaur

Sails to Athens
black sails

Sails to island
Leaves Ariadne

Examples of planning and writing diaries in response to literature

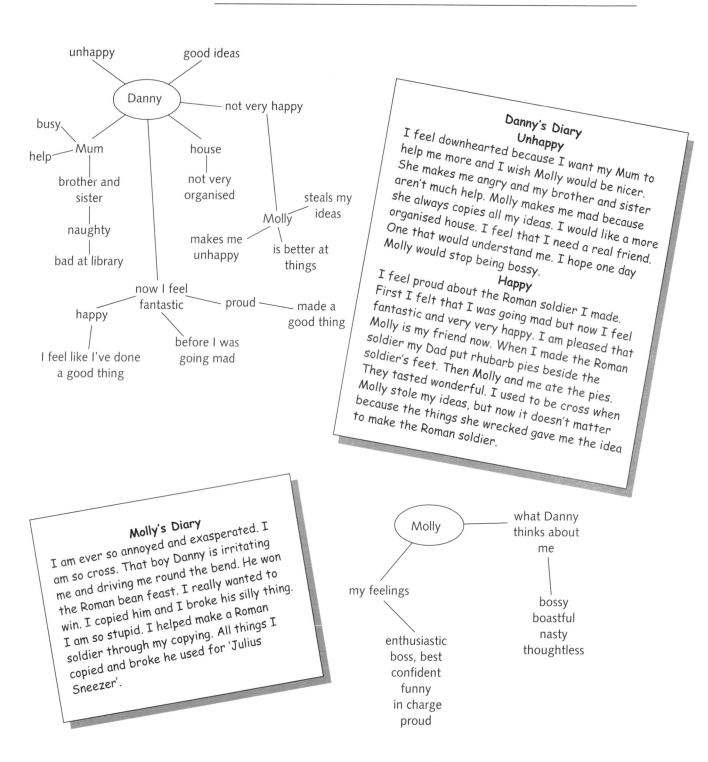

Danny's Diary
Unhappy

I feel downhearted because I want my Mum to help me more and I wish Molly would be nicer. She makes me angry and my brother and sister aren't much help. Molly makes me mad because she always copies all my ideas. I would like a more organised house. I feel that I need a real friend. One that would understand me. I hope one day Molly would stop being bossy.

Happy

I feel proud about the Roman soldier I made. First I felt that I was going mad but now I feel fantastic and very very happy. I am pleased that Molly is my friend now. When I made the Roman soldier my Dad put rhubarb pies beside the soldier's feet. Then Molly and me ate the pies. They tasted wonderful. I used to be cross when Molly stole my ideas, but now it doesn't matter because the things she wrecked gave me the idea to make the Roman soldier.

Molly's Diary

I am ever so annoyed and exasperated. I am so cross. That boy Danny is irritating me and driving me round the bend. He won the Roman bean feast. I really wanted to win. I copied him and I broke his silly thing. I am so stupid. I helped make a Roman soldier through my copying. All things I copied and broke he used for 'Julius Sneezer'.

Stage 2: Introducing the TASC wheel to the whole school

To introduce all the children in the school to the TASC wheel, I chose two activities: writing and art. As well as developing the pupils' problem-solving and thinking skills, a further underlying purpose was to foster the children's emotional intelligence and self-esteem.

Each class worked on these activities at an appropriate level: the teaching approach was the same but obviously both the depth and breadth of the outcomes were different. The aim was to produce visual and language portraits that showed self-understanding.

I made a class wall-chart of the problem-solving wheel with each segment covered with a flap (pp. 114–15). As each stage of the thinking process was discussed and used, the flap was lifted to reveal the questions needed to help with the development of that skill. The process words: gather and organise, identify, generate, decide, implement, evaluate, communicate and learn from experience, were used in all year groups. The children enjoyed using these words and it made the discussion and reflection on the thinking processes much easier.

The mindmap on pages 116–17 shows the general planning for the art activity for Key Stage 1 together with some examples of children's work.

I collected a range of portraits for the children to discuss. We talked about the emotions in the portraits, highlighted methods used to portray feelings and discussed colours and textures in the paintings. The children used a variety of tools to create texture but responded with anxiety when encouraged to mix colours directly on the paper. However, they were given only primary colours and they soon became creative with the paint on the paper. The portraits as a result had extremely rich colours and a liveliness that ready mixed colours often lack. This activity could have been developed by asking the children what other materials they could have used to portray their emotions; for example, collage, clay or paper sculpture.

My reflections on the children's writing

The children responded enthusiastically to the thinking skills wheel and were eager to organise their thoughts about themselves. They all enjoyed using mindmaps to help them to do this.

In Key Stage 1, the children used mindmaps and illustrations to record their ideas and many were able to use their plans to successfully make a poster or a small book. Their response to the whole process was enthusiastic and delightful. If we can model thinking strategies at an early stage, the benefits for the children in their future learning will be tremendous.

In Key Stage 2, the children were so emotionally involved that they preferred not to share their very personal writing with others. However, they were eager to talk about the thinking skills they had used and how these skills had really helped them to plan and express their thoughts clearly. In later weeks, it was very obvious that the children had iternalised the processes of the thinking skills framework since their ability to plan, write and then evaluate their writing improved enormously.

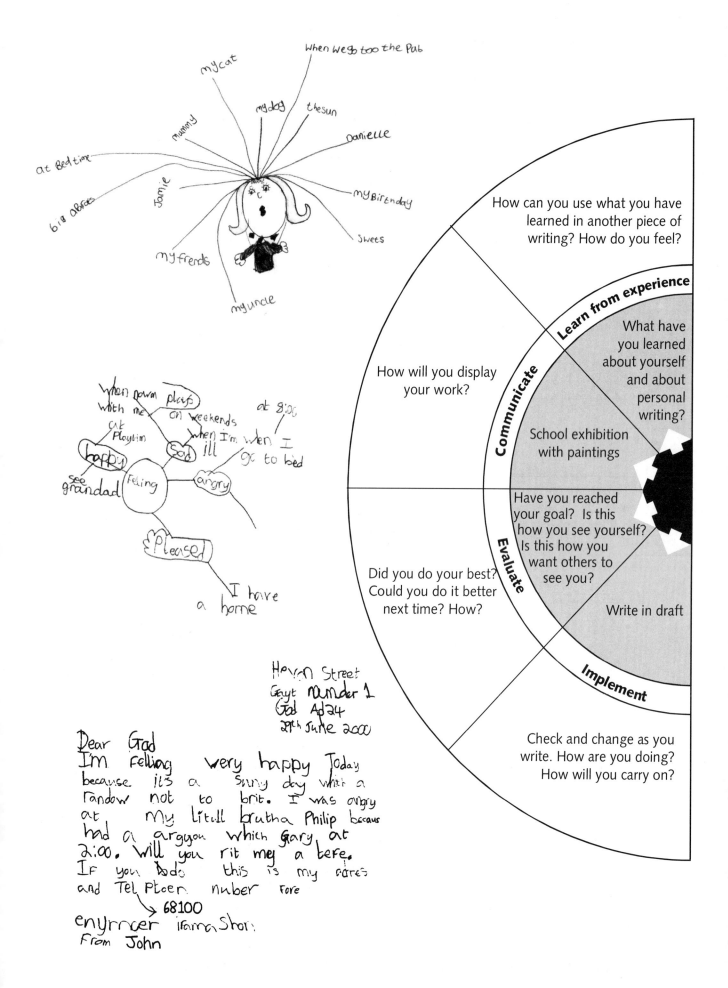

Planning for writing a self-portrait

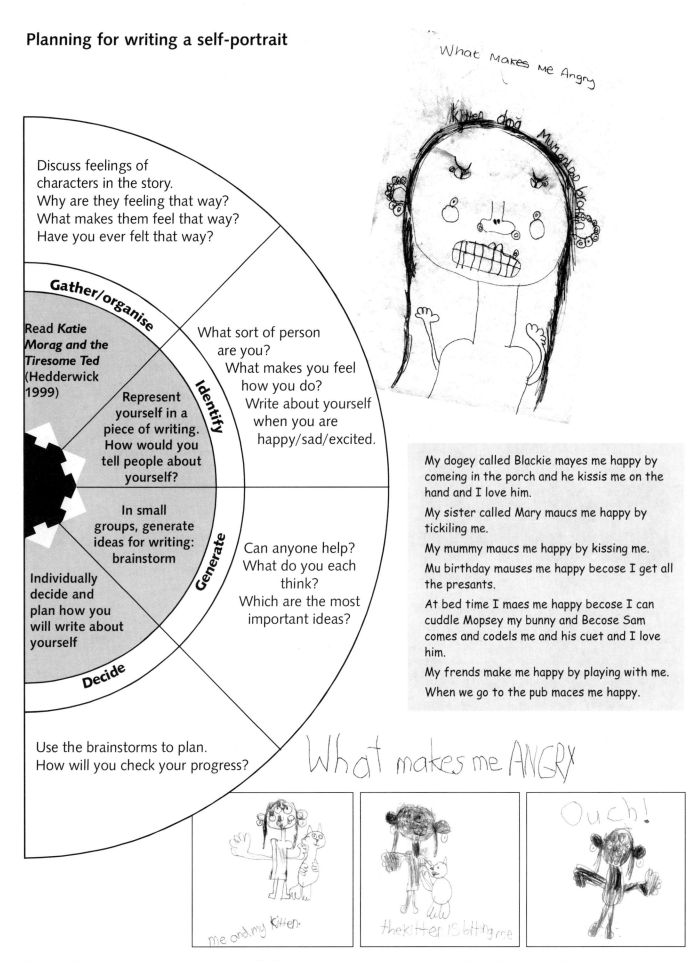

What Makes me Angry

Discuss feelings of characters in the story. Why are they feeling that way? What makes them feel that way? Have you ever felt that way?

Gather/organise

Read *Katie Morag and the Tiresome Ted* (Hedderwick 1999)

Identify

Represent yourself in a piece of writing. How would you tell people about yourself?

What sort of person are you? What makes you feel how you do? Write about yourself when you are happy/sad/excited.

In small groups, generate ideas for writing: brainstorm

Generate

Individually decide and plan how you will write about yourself

Can anyone help? What do you each think? Which are the most important ideas?

Decide

Use the brainstorms to plan. How will you check your progress?

My dogey called Blackie mayes me happy by comeing in the porch and he kissis me on the hand and I love him.

My sister called Mary maucs me happy by tickiling me.

My mummy maucs me happy by kissing me.

Mu birthday mauses me happy becose I get all the presants.

At bed time I maes me happy becose I can cuddle Mopsey my bunny and Becose Sam comes and codels me and his cuet and I love him.

My frends make me happy by playing with me.

When we go to the pub maces me happy.

What makes me ANGRY

me and my kitten.   the kitter is bitting me   Ouch!

Planning for art project: self-portrait

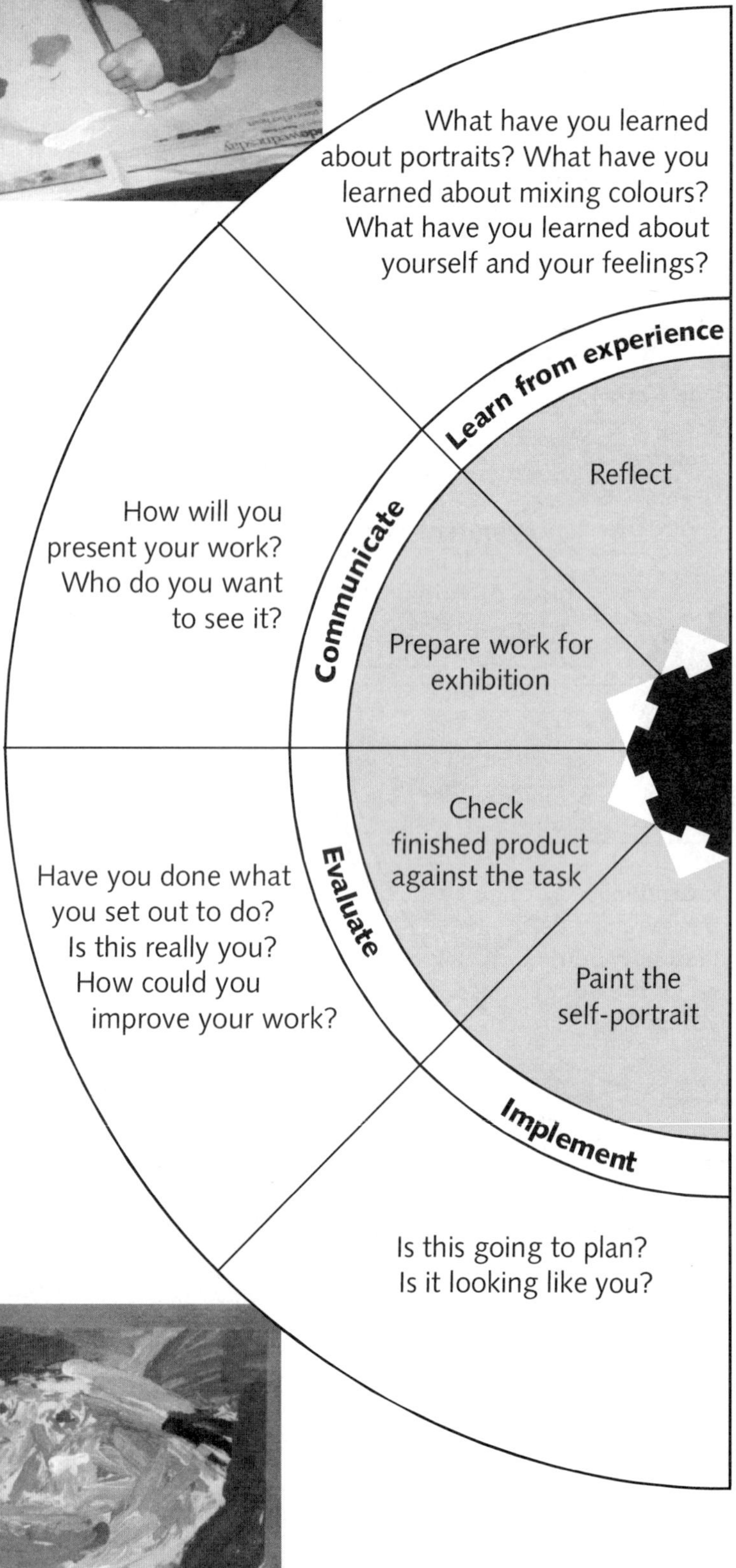

What have you learned about portraits? What have you learned about mixing colours? What have you learned about yourself and your feelings?

Learn from experience

Reflect

Communicate

How will you present your work? Who do you want to see it?

Prepare work for exhibition

Check finished product against the task

Evaluate

Have you done what you set out to do? Is this really you? How could you improve your work?

Paint the self-portrait

Implement

Is this going to plan? Is it looking like you?

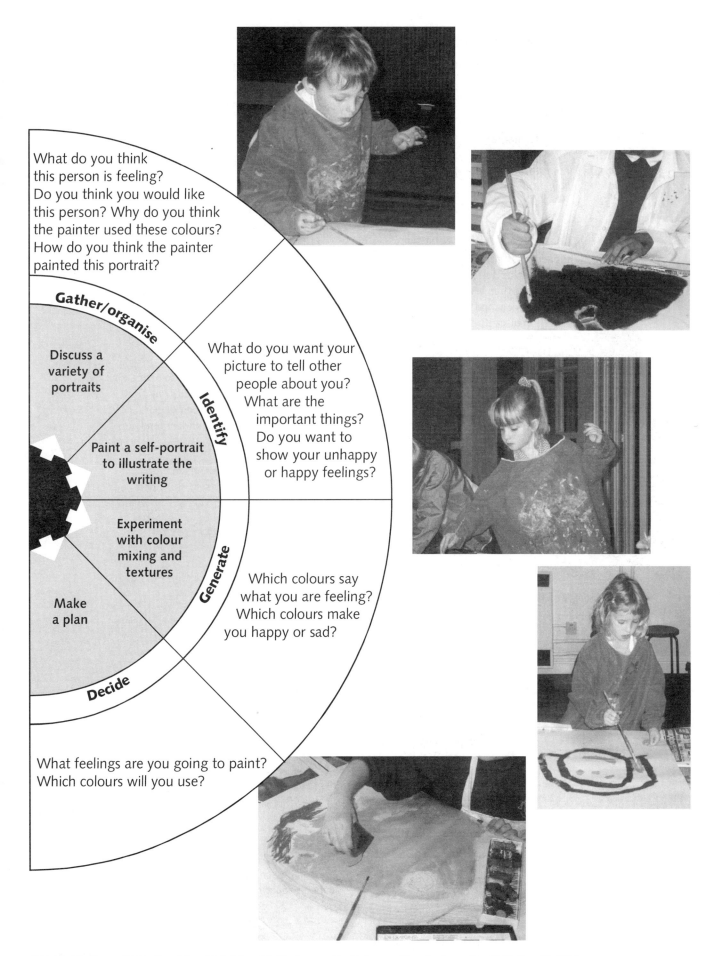

What do you think
this person is feeling?
Do you think you would like
this person? Why do you think
the painter used these colours?
How do you think the painter
painted this portrait?

Gather/organise

Discuss a
variety of
portraits

Identify

Paint a self-portrait
to illustrate the
writing

What do you want your
picture to tell other
people about you?
What are the
important things?
Do you want to
show your unhappy
or happy feelings?

Experiment
with colour
mixing and
textures

Generate

Make
a plan

Which colours say
what you are feeling?
Which colours make
you happy or sad?

Decide

What feelings are you going to paint?
Which colours will you use?

REFLECT *My reflections*

In reflecting on the whole project, a number of key thoughts emerged.

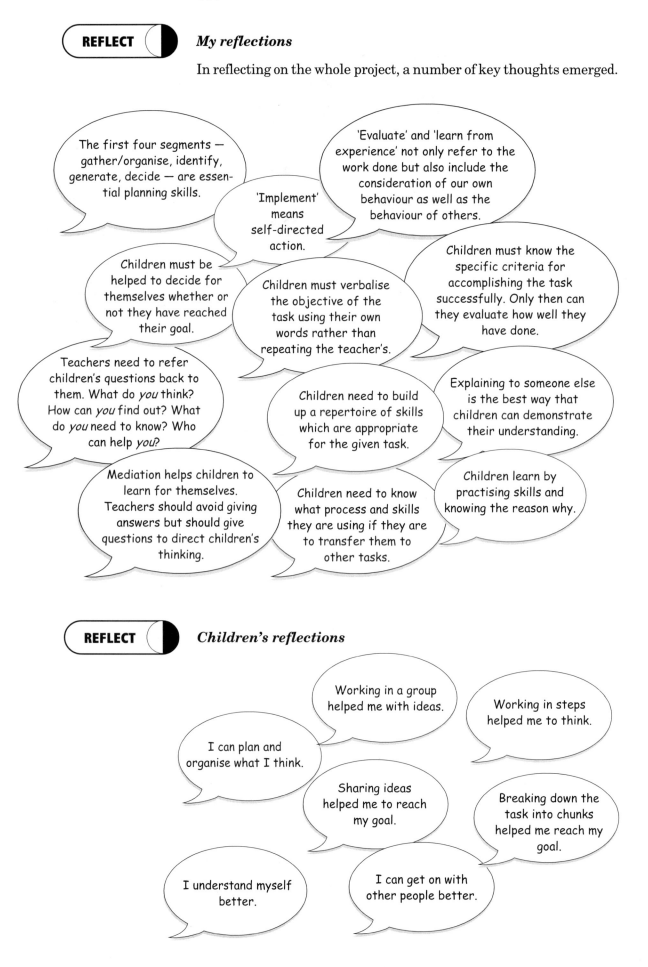

The first four segments — gather/organise, identify, generate, decide — are essential planning skills.

'Implement' means self-directed action.

'Evaluate' and 'learn from experience' not only refer to the work done but also include the consideration of our own behaviour as well as the behaviour of others.

Children must be helped to decide for themselves whether or not they have reached their goal.

Children must verbalise the objective of the task using their own words rather than repeating the teacher's.

Children must know the specific criteria for accomplishing the task successfully. Only then can they evaluate how well they have done.

Teachers need to refer children's questions back to them. What do *you* think? How can *you* find out? What do *you* need to know? Who can help *you*?

Children need to build up a repertoire of skills which are appropriate for the given task.

Explaining to someone else is the best way that children can demonstrate their understanding.

Mediation helps children to learn for themselves. Teachers should avoid giving answers but should give questions to direct children's thinking.

Children need to know what process and skills they are using if they are to transfer them to other tasks.

Children learn by practising skills and knowing the reason why.

REFLECT *Children's reflections*

Working in a group helped me with ideas.

Working in steps helped me to think.

I can plan and organise what I think.

Sharing ideas helped me to reach my goal.

Breaking down the task into chunks helped me reach my goal.

I understand myself better.

I can get on with other people better.

Teachers' reflections

REFLECT

Working in this way motivates, stimulates, clarifies.

This way of working makes it easier to evaluate their writing.

This style of teaching and learning raises children's self-esteem.

I took time to say to myself, 'Now, let me think'.

Inspires children to have original ideas and to think divergently.

Children are enabled to take control and move their own learning forward.

Children are helped to socialise by learning and thinking together.

Thinking creatively is a skill we will need for the future.

Shifts the balance from direct teaching to children motivating themselves.

Having a structure for thinking helps children who are unclear because they are supported by others.

Teaching children thinking skills enables them to master life problems not just curriculum problems.

Sharing ideas frees up thinking because children don't feel inhibited and all contributions are welcome.

Parents' reflections

REFLECT

This project has helped to motivate and organise a lazy boy!

My daughter is able to think things through better. She can see both sides of an argument, action or decision.

My daughter loves to brainstorm and plan her work.

My daughter will often have thought out her argument, or her point of view on everything! Even at teatime she never shuts up!

This way of working has given my son the structure to help him plan successfully.

Conclusion

As teachers, we are continuously learning about children: how they respond to our teaching and how they learn. We all know that they learn by practising skills; and it is important to remind ourselves that we also extend our repertoire of skills by practising. This has certainly been the case for me.

I am even more committed than before to the teaching of problem-solving and thinking skills. The children and the staff have been very receptive and we plan to develop another more extensive whole-school project to consolidate and practise the skills that both teachers and children need.

While reflecting on our work so far, I have discovered a successful way of working for me. I now begin new projects or topics with children by doing a memory search to find out and consolidate what they already know (gathering and organising). This informs me of pupils' prior knowledge and attainment and of what the children need to know and extend further. The focus of my teaching is to fill the gaps with children doing their own research and investigations to fulfil personal challenges; and to lead and extend all this through my direct teaching. We then compare what we have learned at the end of the project with our initial memory search. This produces an excellent record of what has been attained and learned, not only of knowledge but, more importantly, of the skills the children have acquired, i.e. the skills they can use independently. Working with some of the children since the initial projects, I have watched them develop their understanding of, and competency with, the skills and processes they are using. I have been delighted when some children automatically organise their planning and recording in such a way that shows that they are transferring skills, and consequently make steady progress with their learning.

An essential process that enables children to develop their thinking skills and to consolidate the processes and skills they have used is to give them the opportunity to reflect on what they have done and learned. I have given the children in the class I am now working with a learning diary. In this they record weekly activities they have done, who helped them and what they have learned. It is up to the children how much they record but they are encouraged to consider the skills and thinking processes they used. All children are beginning to develop some insight into how they think and learn.

It continues to be a great joy for me to work alongside children who are enjoying the discovery of learning and to offer some guidance on the development of their thinking by taking time to talk with them and taking their ideas seriously. I would encourage teachers to take on the challenge of systematically teaching thinking skills. I am learning all the time from the children's responses and ideas. It is hard work but it is so professionally rewarding.

Examples of questions to help children to develop skills of evaluating and reflecting

Let me stop and THINK!

What have I learned this week? _____

_____

_____

What did I enjoy? Why? _____

_____

_____

What did I do best? _____

_____

_____

What could I have done better? _____

_____

_____

How could I do it better? _____

_____

_____

Who has helped me? How? _____

_____

_____

How did I learn what I learned? _____

_____

_____

Could I use what I have learned in another situation? Can I think of one? _____

_____

_____

What is the most useful thing I learned this week? _____

_____

_____

© Belle Wallace, 2000, *Teaching the Very Able Child*, David Fulton Publishers (reproduced in Wallace 2001, *Teaching Thinking Skills Across the Primary Curriculum*, David Fulton Publishers).

References and useful resources

Literacy

East Riding of Yorkshire Council (1998) *Shaping Thoughts: Models and Frames to Support the Development of Children's Writing*. East Riding of Yorkshire Council.

Dewsbury, A. (1999a) *Assessment Teaching and Learning*, First Steps™ Resource Materials, NLS Edition. Oxford: Ginn Heinemann Professional Development (GHPD).

Dewsbury, A. (1999b) *Information Text Key Stage 1*, First Steps™ Resource Materials, NLS Edition. Oxford: Ginn Heinemann Professional Development (GHPD).

Dewsbury, A. (1999c) *Information Text Key Stage 2*, First Steps™ Resource Materials, NLS Edition. Oxford: Ginn Heinemann Professional Development (GHPD).

Dewsbury, A. (1999d) *Shared and Guided Reading and Writing at Key Stage 1*, First Steps™ Resource Materials, NLS Edition. Oxford: Ginn Heinemann Professional Development (GHPD).

Dewsbury, A. (1999e) *Shared and Guided Reading and Writing at Key Stage 2*, First Steps™ Resource Materials, NLS Edition. Oxford: Ginn Heinemann Professional Development (GHPD).

National Literacy Strategy Activity Resource Banks (1998a) *Module 3 Sentence Level Work*. Oxford: Oxford University Press.

National Literacy Strategy Activity Resource Banks (1998b) *Shared and Guided Reading at KS2*. Oxford: Oxford University Press.

National Literacy Strategy Activity Resource Banks (1998c) *Shared and Guided Reading and Writing at KS1*. Oxford: Oxford University Press.

National Literacy Strategy Activity Resource Banks (1998d) *Reading and Writing for Information*. Oxford: Oxford University Press.

QCA NLS fliers: *The National Literacy Strategy: Grammar for Writing* (ISBN 0 19 312401); *Talking in class* (IBSN 019 312296 0); *Engaging all pupils* (ISBN 0 19 312297 9); *Writing in the Literacy Hour* (ISBN 0 19 312299 5); *Writing to inform* (ISBN 019 312300 2).

Numeracy

Blinko, J. and Graham, N. (1995) *Mathematical Beginnings: Problem Solving for Young Children*. Colchester: Claire Publications.

Blinko, J. and Graham, N. (1997) *Mathematics with Cubes: Problem Solving Activities for Older Children*. Colchester: Claire Publications.

Burton, L. (1984) *Thinking Things Through: Problem Solving in Mathematics*. Oxford: Blackwell.

Casey, R. and Koshy, V. (1995) *Bright Challenge: Learning Activities Specifically Designed for Able Children of all 7–11-year-olds*. Cheltenham: Stanley Thornes.

Clemson, D. and Clemson, W. (1998) *Blueprints: Maths Investigations*. Cheltenham: Nelson Thornes.

Davis, J. and Tibbatts, S. (1994) *Maths Puzzles*. Leamington Spa: Scholastic.

Fisher, R. and Vince, A. (1989a) *Investigating Maths, Book 2*. Oxford: Blackwell.

Fisher, R. and Vince, A. (1989b) *Investigating Maths, Book 3*. Oxford: Blackwell.

Fisher, R. and Vince, A. (1989c) *Investigating Maths, Book 4*. Oxford: Blackwell.

Frood, K. and Deale, S. (1992) *Using and Applying Maths: Number*. Oxford: Heinemann.

Graham, E. (1990) *Mathematics for Teddy Bears*. Colchester: Claire Publications.

Hyams, S. M. (1993) *Challenges for Children*. Colchester: Claire Publications.

Kanter, P. and Gillespie, J. (1996) *Nelson Connect: Partner Games*. Cheltenham: Nelson.

Kirkby, D. (1992a) *Creative Maths 7–9*. Dunstable: Folens.

Kirkby, D. (1992b) *Creative Maths 9–11*. Dunstable: Folens.

Kirkby, D. (1992c) *Spectrum Maths: Starting Algebra / Shape and Space*. London: Collins Educational.

Kirkby, D. (1995a) *Spectrum Maths: Starting Investigations*. London: Collins Educational.

Kirkby, D. (1995b) *Spectrum Maths: More Investigations*. London: Collins Educational.

Kirkby, D. (1996a) *Spectrum Maths: Go Further with Investigations*. London: Collins Educational.

Kirkby, D. (1996b) *Spectrum Maths: Go Further with Data Handling*. London: Collins Educational.

Kirkby, D. (1996c) *Spectrum Maths: Go Further with Games*. London: Collins Educational.

Kirkby, D. (1999) *Spectrum Maths: Teacher's Book Number 6*. London: Collins Educational.

Langdon, N. and Snape, C. (1984) *A Way with Maths*. Cambridge: Cambridge University Press.

Murchison, J. (1999) *Maths Problems for Gifted and Talented Students*. Colchester: Claire Publications.

O'Brien, T. (1992) *Problems, Challenges and Investigations*. Colchester: Claire Publications.

Prim-Ed Publishing (1996) *Maths Problems Galore*. Nuneaton: Prim-Ed Publishing.

Snape, C. and Scott, H. (2000) *Puzzles, Mazes and Numbers*. Cambridge: Cambridge University Press.

Straker, A. (1993) *Talking Points in Mathematics*. Cambridge: Cambridge University Press.

Webber, B. and Haigh, J. (1989) *Let's Investigate Numbers*. Leamington Spa: Scholastic.

Science

Beasley, G. and Pengelly, B. (1999) *Science, Key Stage 1, Scottish levels A–B.* Leamington Spa: Scholastic.

Cuthbert, K. (1998) *Discoveries: Creative Projects to Promote Science, Design and Language Skills with Children from Five to Eleven Years.* Dunstable: Belair.

Feasey, R. (1999) *Primary Science and Literacy.* Hatfield: Association for Science Education.

Feasey, R. and Gallear, B. (2000) *Primary Science and Numeracy.* Hatfield: Association for Science Education.

Feasey, R. and Siraj-Blatchford, J. (1998) *Key Skills: Communication in Science.* Durham: University of Durham.

Keogh, B. and Naylor, S. *Starting Points for Science.* Sandbach: Millgate House.

Kirk, S. (1999) *Science, Key Stage 2, Scottish levels C–E.* Leamington Spa: Scholastic.

Lewis, M. and Wray, D. (1996) *Writing Frames: Scaffolding Children's Non-fiction Writing in a Range of Genres.* Reading: University of Reading, Reading and Language Information Centre.

Lewis, M. and Wray, D. (1998) *Writing Across the Curriculum: Frames to Support Learning.* Reading: University of Reading, Reading and Language Information Centre.

Palmer, P. (ed.) *Science Challenges: Practical Activities for Able Children in KS2.* Hertfordshire: Nuffield Foundation and Hertfordshire County Council.

Parkin, T. and Lewis, M. (eds) (1998) *Science and Literacy: A Guide for Primary Teachers.* London: Collins Educational for the Nuffield Foundation.

General references

Adams, H. B. (1986) 'Teaching general problem-solving strategies in the classroom', *Gifted Education International* 4(2), 84–9.

ATM (2000) *Mathematical Puzzles.* Derby: ATM.

Bentley, R. A. (1995) 'Able Thinkers Learning', *Flying High* Spring, 10–18.

Department for Education and Employment (DfEE) (1998) *The Autumn Package of Pupil Performance.* London: DfEE.

Department for Education and Employment (DfEE) (1999a) *National Numeracy Strategy Framework for Teaching Mathematics from Reception to Year 6.* London: DfEE.

Department for Education and Employment (DfEE) (1999b) *Guide for Your Professional Development: Book 4, Raising Standards with Early Years, in Key Stage 1 and in Special Schools.* London: DfEE.

Department for Education and Employment (DfEE) (2000a) *National Literacy and Numeracy Strategies: Guidance on Teaching Able Children.* London: DfEE.

Department for Education and Employment (DfEE) (2000b) *National Numeracy Strategy, Framework for Teaching Mathematics in Year 7.* London: DfEE.

Fisher, R. and Vince, A. (1989a) *Investigating Maths, Book 2.* Oxford: Blackwell.

Fisher, R. and Vince, A. (1989a) *Investigating Maths, Book 2.* Oxford: Blackwell.

Fisher, R. and Vince, A. (1989b) *Investigating Maths, Book 3.* Oxford: Blackwell.

Fisher, R. and Vince, A. (1989c) *Investigating Maths, Book 4.* Oxford: Blackwell.

Freeman, J. (1998) *Educating the Very Able: Current International Research.* London: The Stationery Office.

Hedderwick, Mairi (illus.) (1999) *Katie Morag and the Tiresome Ted.* London: Red Fox.

Lake, M. and Needham, M. (1995) *Top Ten Thinking Tactics: A Practical Introduction to the Thinking Skills Revolution.* Birmingham: Questions Publishing Company.

Langdon, N. and Snape, C. (1984) *A Way with Maths.* Cambridge: Cambridge University Press.

Lewis, M. and Wray, D. (1997) *Writing Frames: Scaffolding Children's Non-

fiction Writing in a Range of Genres. Reading: University of Reading, Reading and Language Information Centre.

Office for Standards in Education (OFSTED) (1994) *Improving Schools*. London: The Stationery Office..

Office for Standards in Education (OFSTED) (1998) *Reviews of Research-Educating the Very Able: Current International Research*.London: The Stationery Office.

Sternberg, R. J. (1985) *Beyond IQ: A Triarchic Theory of Human Intelligence*. Cambridge: Cambridge University Press.

Vygotsky, L. S. (1978) *Mind in Society: The Development of Higher Psychological Processes,* M. Cole *et al.* (eds). Cambridge, Mass.: Harvard University Press.

Wallace, B. (2000) *Teaching the Very Able Child: Developing a Policy and Adopting Strategies for Provision*. London: David Fulton Publishers.

Wallace, B. and Adams, H. B. (1993) *TASC: Thinking Actively in a Social Context*. Oxford: AB Academic Publishers.

Wallace, B. and Bentley, R. A. (eds) (in press) *Teaching Thinking Skills Across The Curriculum: A Practical Approach for Middle Years*. London: David Fulton Publishers.

Williams, S. and Wegerif, R. (2000a) *Teaching Thinking*, Spring 2000. Birmingham: Questions Publishing Company.

Williams, S. and Wegerif, R. (2000b) *Teaching Thinking*, Autumn 2000. Birmingham: Questions Publishing Company.

Websites for teachers

Association of Teachers of Mathematics
http://acorn.educ.nottingham.ac.uk/SchEd/pages/atm/

Association for Science Education
www.asc.org.uk

National Centre for Literacy and Numeracy
www.standards.dfee.gov.uk

National Grid for Learning
www.ngfl.gov.uk

NRICH Online Maths Project
www.nrich.maths.org.uk

Qualifications and Curriculum Authority
www.qca.org.uk

Standards Unit of the DFEE
www.standards.dfee/literacy.gov.uk

Index